Contents

Dedication	IV
Preface	V
Introduction	VII
1. Importance of Vision	1
2. Vision Impairement	7
3. Catch the Vision	12
4. A Vision of Your New Identity	26
5. Confirm the Vision	37
6. Execute the Vision	46
7. Protect the Vision	55
8. Execution Boosters (The 7 P's)	73
9. Goal Planning Template	101
Epilogue	114
Contact the Author	115
A Sinner's Prayer	116
About the Author	117

Dedication

This book is dedicated to those who thrive on challenging the status quo. They are the dreamers, who challenge themselves and others to always innovate and continuously improve.

It is dedicated to those who consistently ensure that their God-given vision is executed. They are the visionaries, who judiciously pay the price to bring to realization God's will on earth, as it is in heaven.

It is dedicated to you, who have decided to read this book, so that you can keep dreaming like a child, but keep executing your dreams like a professional.

Finally, this book is dedicated to the Father of our Lord Jesus Christ, who said, *"Let us make man in our own image and likeness,"* and excellently executed on that vision.

Preface

Vision, in the biblical context, is the unfolding of divine plan and purpose. Everyone is created to fulfill a purpose here on earth. Just as every manufacturer produces a product to achieve a specific purpose, God created us for a purpose. A discovery of that purpose for which you were created is called vision. The vision for your life can also be understood as God's dream for you.

While they might seem similar, there is a world of difference between vision and ambition. **Vision is God-given, whereas ambition is man-made.** Vision is from above, while ambition has its origin here on earth. Ambition is born out of covetousness, envy, a desire for power and recognition, and a drive to outshine others. Vision, on the other hand, is born out of a realization of what God's will for mankind is and the part He wants you to play in bringing it to fruition. Adolf Hitler had the ambition to conquer Europe, while George Muller had the vision to preserve the destiny of homeless children.

Vision is what we see with our spiritual eyes. That is why David prayed in Psalms 119:18, *"Open my eyes, that I may see wondrous things from Your law."*

You can only become what you see, and you can only create what you have seen. In creation, God already knew the finished state and what it would take to get there.

As you read this book, may God's plan for your life be clear for you to see and understand. May this book be salve in your eyes, causing you to see God's glorious plan for your life. If you already know an aspect of God's plan for your life, I pray that the next phase will be revealed to you.

The Holy Spirit is the safest gateway to the supernatural realm. Any believer who carries the presence of the Holy Spirit is also a gateway to the supernatural realm. This is why Jesus told the disciples to tell the people that the Kingdom of God has come near to them (Luke 10:9). Jesus preached the same message Himself (Mark 1:15). In like manner, a word from a carrier of the Holy Spirit is a gateway to the supernatural realm. This book was born of the Spirit of God; therefore, expect supernatural manifestations as you digest the contents of this book.

Introduction

Vision is the ability to see. Physical vision, though very important, dwarfs in comparison to the importance of having a vision for one's life. Every vision from God has an unlimited capacity to deliver results. This is why knowing your assignment and vision determines your life placement.

There is a huge gap between having a compelling vision and successfully executing it. Those who have learned to dream might not realize their dreams because they fail in execution. No matter how great your vision is, without execution, it will simply be a wish.

Jesus said that to enter the kingdom of God, we must be like little children (Matthew 18:3). On the other hand, Jesus also said that the same kingdom of God suffers violence and that violent people must take it by force (Matthew 11:12). The last time I checked, little children are less likely to be violent or to take things by force. Entering the kingdom of God requires dreaming like a child; however, staying and dominating in the kingdom requires executing the vision like a mature believer, a professional. An excellently executed vision will lead to a glorious destiny.

Every vision has an unlimited capacity to energize the visioner. You must spend enough time reading and meditating on your vision's possibilities before the passion rises within you.

The vision referred to in this book is different from vision as a way God can speak to you. God can speak to His children in a variety of ways. He can talk to His children through dreams, directly to our human spirit, a voice from heaven, visions, etc. In this regard, a vision is a picture or video God shows us. He can use this means to communicate with us. It could be a past, current, or future occurrence. The vision can come while we are awake and conscious (open-eyed vision) or awake but unconscious (trance).

However, the vision referred to in this book is the awareness of the destination that God has communicated to us for different aspects of our lives or our lives as a whole. God can communicate His vision for our lives through several means, which will be explored in this book.

Vision addresses the "*where*" of a person's life, while purpose addresses the *"why"* of a person's vision. A strategy addresses the *"how," "who,"* and *"when"* of a person's vision.

Open your heart to God as you read the words in this book. Expect divine visitations, visions and God-breathed strategies as you *eat* the words in this book.

1
Importance of Vision

Vision is the ability to see ahead. Helen Keller said, "*The only thing worse than being blind is having sight but no vision.*"

The context of vision we are exploring here is the ability to see a future for your life. It is the ability to see the destination God has ordained for you. It may be a future for your career, your marriage, your ministry, your children, etc. Without vision, people cast off restraint and they are eventually destroyed (Proverbs 29:18 KJV).

The lack of a compelling vision can make people avoid savings or investments. The lack of a compelling vision will make a person to continually make the wrong choice of friends, spouse, etc. A lack of vision can cause a woman to remain in an abusive relationship. Furthermore, it can cause a person to remain in the employment of an abusive employer.

ADVANTAGES OF HAVING A COMPELLING VISION

A Faith Booster

Vision is one of the main ingredients of hope. Hope is needed to have faith; faith is needed to please God. Without vision, there is nothing to look forward to when the going gets tough. There is nothing to cause you to keep pressing ahead when the going is good. The future belongs to those who can see it. During one of Abraham's numerous encounters with God, God told him to step outside and count the number of stars in the sky. The act of counting the stars created a vision of him with all his descendants in his mind. It is noted that this caused Abraham to believe. Perhaps what is hindering your faith from growing is the lack of a compelling vision from God.

Then He brought him outside and said, "Look now toward heaven, and count the stars if you are able to number them." And He said to him, "So shall your descendants be." And he believed in the Lord, and He accounted it to him for righteousness. (Genesis 15:5-6)

In another instance, God told Abraham to look towards the north, south, east and west to catch a vision of his descendants occupying the land he was dwelling in. God also told him to walk through the land. All these instructions from God were designed to boost Abraham's faith.

And the Lord said to Abram, after Lot had separated from him: "Lift your eyes now and look from the place where you are—northward, southward, eastward, and westward; for all the land which you see I give to you and your descendants forever. And I will make your descendants as the dust of the earth; so that if a man could number the dust of the earth, then your descendants also could be numbered. Arise, walk in the land through its length and its width, for I give it to you." (Genesis 13:14-17)

Since we cannot receive answers from God without faith (Mark 11:24), vision is crucial for us to build our faith. We also cannot have faith without hope. In defining faith, the Bible says, *"Now faith is the substance of things hoped for, the evidence of things not seen."* (Hebrews 11:1) It means that if you do not hope for anything, you cannot have faith. Vision is a compelling picture of our future, and this then causes us to hope for something. You see, if we want to have hope and strengthen our faith in God, it is absolutely important to have a compelling vision from God.

Lasting Success

Success is made up of a culmination of right decisions a person or group has made. There is no lasting success without vision. God regularly made use of the ministry of Prophets to instill a vision in the hearts of His children. This is because He wanted them to be successful.

There will always come a time in a person's life when they will need to make decisions. The decisions become difficult when there seems to be success regardless of the direction they go. The Bible says, *"There is a way that seems right to a man, but its end is the way of death."* (Proverbs 14:12) A compelling vision for the future is what guides the decisions that a person will make. If as a student, you have a vision of being the best in your class, this vision will make it easy for you to decide to study, when your friends are going partying. If as a Christian, you have a vision of pleasing God, deciding to live holy will be easy.

A compelling vision energizes the visioner to keep making decisions that will lead to the attainment of that vision. Even secular organizations have caught onto this. Every leading organization has a compelling vision for the future. It is on record that when World War II had ended, Robert Woodruff, the CEO of Coca Cola at that time, stated that their vision was for every person in the world to have a taste of Coca Cola. With careful planning and lots of persistence, this vision was achieved.

True success can be defined as the attainment of the God-given vision. Jesus Christ was successful. John the Baptist was successful. Joseph was successful. Joshua was successful. Daniel was successful, etc. True success is not how much money you have, neither is it how many houses or cars you have. These things are man-made measures of success. Before God, you and I will be judged based on how well we become who God called us to be, and how well we did what God called us to do. May you be successful in Jesus' name.

Longevity

Without a compelling vision, life is not worth living. Many people lose the will to live, because they do not see anything compelling to live for. There are people that are successful for a little while; their success does not seem to last long. To a large extent, it is because they lack a compelling vision.

King Solomon started his reign with a vision to see the temple of God built. After that was completed, the next vision was to build a palace for the King. Once those two compelling visions were achieved, there was nothing else Solomon was pursuing. You will never see in scriptures where Solomon was pursuing the actualization of any other compelling vision. Hence, the rest of Solomon's reign was a colossal failure. The man of whom it was once said, *"And Solomon loved the Lord, walking in the statutes of David his father: only he sacrificed and burnt incense in high places"* (1 Kings 3:3), now became a man that did evil in the sight of the Lord (1 Kings 11:6).

You can never arrive at a future you did not see. People that attain success will tell you that they saw it coming. The same goes with longevity. Visionaries focus on things others do not see. This is what drives them. It causes them to outlast every challenge and difficulty. Read what the Bible has to say about this.

Therefore we do not lose heart. Even though our outward man is perishing, yet the inward man is being renewed day by day. For our light affliction, which is but for a moment, is working for us a far more exceeding and eternal weight of glory, **while we do not look at the things which are seen, but at the things which are not seen. For the things which are seen are temporary, but the things which are not seen are eternal.** *(2 Corinthians 4:16-18)*

Ask God to open your eyes to see the future He has ordained for you. Yours will be different from mine. God is faithful, He will answer your prayers.

Apostle Paul's vision from God enabled him to outlast tough times. It enabled him to always know that he still had a future. When he was shipwrecked, he was undaunted, because he knew the vision God gave him had not been fully accomplished. The Apostles (Peter and John) were able to resist the intimidation tactics of the religious leaders because of what they had seen.

But Peter and John answered and said to them, "Whether it is right in the sight of God to listen to you more than to God, you judge. For we cannot but speak the things which we have seen and heard." (Acts 4:20)

Until you have finished attaining the compelling vision God has given to you, you are indestructible. Until you retire from God's vision for your life, you are still in God's service. No one in God's service can be taken out by the devil. Vision guarantees longevity.

2

Vision Impairement

Just like a person's physical eyes can become defective, a person's ability to see ahead can also become defective. It is important to understand this, so we know how to accurately diagnose the state of our vision. We will examine **four distinct vision defects** and how they can be corrected.

VISION DEFECTS

Blindness

Vision blindness is a condition where a person is unable to see God's plan for their lives. The main causes of blindness are rebellion and having a hardened heart towards God. Blindness could be either complete or partial.

The Apostles were scolded by Jesus Christ, because they were still doubtful of His ability to do miracles, even though they had seen Him perform miracles. Jesus diagnosed that their lack of perception and blindness was because of a hardened heart.

But Jesus, being aware of it, said to them, "Why do you reason because you have no bread? Do you not yet perceive or understand? Is your heart still hardened? Having eyes, do you not see? And having ears, do you not hear? And do you not remember? (Mark 8:17-18)

The children of Israel were also scolded by God, and He was going to punish them for the evil they had done in His sight. Just like the Apostles, they were diagnosed with blindness, though they had physical sight. God declared through the prophet Jeremiah, *"Hear this now, O foolish people, without understanding, who have eyes and see not, and who have ears and hear not"* (Jeremiah 5:21). Reading further, we see why they were blind. Jeremiah 5:23 reads, *"But this people has a defiant and rebellious heart; they have revolted and departed."*

We also see the same diagnosis repeated in Ezekiel 12:2. It reads: *"Son of man, you dwell in the midst of a rebellious house, which has eyes to see but does not see, and ears to hear but does not hear; for they are a rebellious house."*

Rebellion is a dangerous state to be in. This is what caused Lucifer to lose his exalted position in heaven. Whenever you find yourself unwilling to be under spiritual authority, you are inviting vision blindness. If you find that you just resent being instructed and directed by people higher than you, it is an indication that you are battling with rebellion. Ask God to forgive you, and immediately rebuke the operation of the spirit of rebellion in your life. Swiftly submit yourself to God, both directly and indirectly (through His human delegated spiritual authority). To further understand what spiritual authority means, and how to locate a spiritual authority to submit to, read the book I authored, *"The Blessings of Being Under Spiritual Authority."*

Vision blindness can also come from living in darkness. Every unbeliever is under the sway of the devil (1 John 5:19). The devil is capable of blinding their eyes from seeing God's plan for their lives. The devil is ruler over the kingdom of darkness. It is difficult to see while in darkness, but there is also the kind of darkness that it is impossible to see from. If you are reading this book, you are neither born again nor truly walking with God, chances are that you are vision blind. Until you renounce sin and accept Jesus Christ as your Lord and savior, you will never be able to clearly see God's plan for your life. If you want to come back home to God right now, please go to the end of the book and sincerely repeat the sinner's prayer. Be delivered from the blinding power of the devil now in Jesus' name.

But even if our gospel is veiled, it is veiled to those who are perishing, whose minds the god of this age has blinded, who do not believe, lest the light of the gospel of the glory of Christ, who is the image of God, should shine on them. (2 Corinthians 4:3-4)

Short-Sightedness

Another vision defect is short-sightedness. This is a condition where people do not see too far off in the future. They are unable to see further than 3, 6, 12, 24 months, etc. They have the mindset of "*Let us eat and drink, for tomorrow we die*" (Isaiah 22:13). They are unable to see as far as 5, 10, 20, 30, 40, 50, 100 years, etc.

Long-Sightedness

Other people have the vision condition that I call long-sightedness. They are only able to see far away. They do not see things within a shorter time frame. They are always focusing on what will happen in the future, without planning for the near future. They think only about 10, 20, 30, 40, 50, 100 years, etc. Yes, it is important to think about the future, but it is also necessary for an individual to stop and smell the roses.

God even tells us to learn from the ants. They have the ability to prepare for the short-term. They prepare their bread in summer and gather their food in harvest. They understand the short-term cycle that will ensure their survival and ability to hit long-term targets.

"Go to the ant, O sluggard; consider her ways, and be wise. Without having any chief, officer, or ruler, she prepares her bread in summer and gathers her food in harvest." (Proverbs 6:6-8)

Not only do we need to plan for the next generation, we also need to care for the current generation. A person that is starving themselves, just to prepare for a future they might not even live to see, is not acting wisely. There must be a proper balance between being short-sighted and long-sighted.

Blurred Vision

Unlike the other conditions, this condition can be difficult to detect. It is the kind of vision where the visionary is deceived. This is critical, because the visionary actually thinks they have the right vision, but in reality, they do not. They are under the influence of the spirit of delusion. Let us examine Revelation 3:17-18 to get more insight on this.

Because you say, 'I am rich, have become wealthy, and have need of nothing'—and do not know that you are wretched, miserable, poor, blind, and naked— I counsel you to buy from Me gold refined in the fire, that you may be rich; and white garments, that you may be clothed, that the shame of your nakedness may not be revealed; and anoint your eyes with eye salve, that you may see.

This Church thought they were rich, wealthy and had need of nothing, but in reality, they were wretched, miserable, poor, blind and naked before

God. How is this possible? The Bible tells us, *"For as he thinks in his heart, so is he. 'Eat and drink!' he says to you, but his heart is not with you."* (Proverbs 23:7) The cause of vision blurriness are things like covetousness, envy, jealousy, bitterness, etc. When infected by these, the victim can begin to believe a lie.

The cure for this is to believe the truth in God's word. We are victorious when we fight the good fight of faith in order to hold on to what God has said. If God says forgive, then you ought to forgive. If God says you should head to the north, then to the north it is. This kind of attitude towards God's word will preserve your vision and shield you from anything that might cause your vision to be blurred.

"And with all unrighteous deception among those who perish, because they did not receive the love of the truth, that they might be saved. And for this reason God will send them strong delusion, that they should believe the lie, that they all may be condemned who did not believe the truth but had pleasure in unrighteousness." (2 Thessalonians 2:10-12)

If you are covetous, envious, jealous, bitter, etc. mostly likely the vision you have is not from God. It is not too late to be right. Repent, and go back to God to get His true vision for your life.

3
Catch the Vision

In medical science, one of the questions usually asked when diagnosing a patient is whether a particular disease or illness is in their lineage. If it is, there is a likelihood that the patient might have it, too.

In spiritual matters, when desiring a particular gift or character trait, we need to find out whether such is in our Spiritual DNA. For example, in order to desire to see the invisible or to see ahead, we must first find out if this is a characteristic that our Heavenly Father has.

God Himself said in Isaiah 46:10, *"Declaring the end from the beginning, and from ancient times things that are not yet done, Saying, 'My counsel shall stand, And I will do all My pleasure.'"* This shows that God can see and declare the end from the beginning. This means God is a visioner.

Haggai called God, the God that Sees. We see this in Genesis 16:13, *"Then she called the name of the LORD who spoke to her, You-Are-the-God-Who-Sees; for she said, 'Have I also here seen Him who sees me?'"*

From these two passages, we see that our progenitor, God, can see ahead. This means we also have the innate (by spiritual birth) ability to see ahead. Praise God!

Ways to Discover God's Plan For Your Life

The Word of God

We can catch God's vision for our lives through the Word of God. This can be either the written Word of God (logos) or the revealed Word of God (rhema).

The Bible tells us, *"Then the LORD appeared again in Shiloh. For the LORD revealed Himself to Samuel in Shiloh by the word of the LORD."* (I Samuel 3:21) God can reveal Himself through His word.

The Word of God is one of the entry points into the supernatural. One of the ways that I know a minister is anointed is whether God begins to speak to me while the minister is teaching. When preached with the power of the Holy Spirit, the Word of God has a calming effect on a person's spirit. In most cases, a child of God who does not clearly hear from God is simply in that condition because they are not able to focus on God. This is perhaps why God resorts to speaking to people while they are asleep, through dreams. For us to get revelations through the Word of God, our hearts and minds must be connected, just like a body of water needs to be still before you can clearly see your reflection.

There are vision capsules from Genesis to Revelation. God does not change. His strategy for you to achieve His vision for your life might be different, but our vision is not too far from examples in Scripture. God will elevate some believers to positions of power and authority like Joseph; God will use some believers like Apostle Paul; and some believers will be great prophets like Elijah. Until eternity, the vision God gave Bible characters will be repeated in our lives.

Catching God's vision for our lives is not new. John the Baptist found his vision in the Word of God. He located the words of prophecy that Isaiah spoke in Isaiah 40:3. While that Scripture was revealed to him, it struck a chord in him, and he just knew that the prophecy was referring to him.

He said: "I am 'the voice of one crying in the wilderness: "make straight the way of the Lord,"'' as the prophet Isaiah said." (John 1:23)

Jesus Christ also located God's vision for Him in the Word of God. This account is in Luke 4:17-20.

And He was handed the book of the prophet Isaiah. And when He had opened the book, He found the place where it was written: "The Spirit of the Lord is upon Me, because He has anointed Me to preach the gospel to the poor; He has sent Me to heal the brokenhearted, to proclaim liberty to the captives and recovery of sight to the blind, to set at liberty those who are oppressed; to proclaim the acceptable year of the Lord. "Then He closed the book, and gave it back to the attendant and sat down. And the eyes of all who were in the synagogue were fixed on Him. And He began to say to them, "Today this Scripture is fulfilled in your hearing."

Jesus Christ and John the Baptist located their vision in the Word of God. This is a very powerful tool for discovering the vision God has for us. Believers ought not to relegate the Word of God to a book that is only opened in Church on Sundays.

When reading the Word of God, we must understand that it is the equivalent of sitting with Jesus Christ and asking Him questions or listening to Him read us a story. The written Word of God is God. Meditate on John 1:1 until it sticks in your heart that Jesus Christ is the Word of God. It states thus: *"In the beginning was the Word, and the Word was with God, and the Word was God."* You can have unfettered access to God anytime and anywhere if you interact with God's Word in spirit and truth.

Empowered to See

The Word of God can open our eyes to see. Naturally, words have the power to kindle our imaginations. God's word has an even more powerful ability to form pictures, imaginations and desires in our hearts. When speaking with His children, God begins by saying "behold" or "see". He is simply saying that we should picture what He is saying. In Joshua 6:2, it is written, *"And the LORD said to Joshua: 'See! I have given Jericho into your hand, its king, and the mighty men of valor.'"* We also see something similar in 1 Samuel 3:11, *"Then the LORD said to Samuel: 'Behold, I will do something in Israel at which both ears of everyone who hears it will tingle.'"* Hence, we can catch a vision from God's words. The Word of God indeed empowers us to see. Often, when God speaks concerning our future, the words He says immediately transform into images and/or video and become real. An example is in Isaiah 2:1, *"The word that Isaiah the son of Amoz saw concerning Judah and Jerusalem."*

Settle down and locate Scriptures concerning any area of your life where you desire to see God's plan, and you will catch a vision.

The Holy Spirit

The Holy Spirit can reveal God's plan for our lives. God wants us to know His plan. The Holy Spirit is the safest way to experience supernatural occurrences. The Holy Spirit gives us access to God's breaking news. He helps us know what God is saying to us in the now.

"But God has revealed them to us through His Spirit. For the Spirit searches all things, yes, the deep things of God. For what man knows the things of a man except the spirit of the man which is in him? Even so no one knows the things of God except the Spirit of God. Now we have received, not the spirit of the world, but the Spirit who is from God, that we might know the things that have been freely given to us by God." (1 Corinthians 2:10-12)

The Holy Spirit is like a search engine that gives believers access to the information residing in God. With the right search queries, we can get access to the information that we seek. God wants you to know his vision for your life. The Holy Spirit can reveal that to you if you pay the price for access.

Every born-again Christian has the right to be filled with the Holy Spirit. If you are not sure you are filled with the Holy Spirit, ask God. He will freely give you the Holy Spirit. If you are unsure why you need the Holy Spirit, read the book of Acts in the Bible to see how the Holy Spirit helped the believers fulfil their destiny. You can be baptized in the Holy Spirit by asking God directly, listening to an anointed message or the laying on hands by someone baptized in the Holy Spirit. To learn more about this topic, read my book, *"Now That You Are Born Again, What Next?"*

Once you are baptized in the Holy Spirit, you can begin engaging the Holy Spirit for the answers you seek.

God can use the ministry of the Holy Spirit to reveal His plan for our lives. That plan can be revealed through a dream (e.g. Joseph - Genesis 37); it could be revealed through a vision (e.g. Apostle Paul - Acts 26:19); it could also be revealed through the voice of God (e.g. Apostle John - Revelation 1:10). Apostle John was ***"in the Spirit"*** when he heard the voice that spoke to him. Therefore, to receive from the Holy Spirit, we have to be in the Holy Spirit and the Holy Spirit in us.

A believer who has learned to worship God will always have an audience with God (John 4:23). A believer who has learned how to pray in the Holy Spirit consistently will always get breaking news from God in their inbox (1 Corinthians 2:10-16).

Once you know how to follow the steps to connect with the Holy Spirit, ensure that you take time to be quiet and listen. Communication is a two-way street. After prayer and/or worship, practice being still to read any message that might be in your inbox, so to speak. We are told in Psalms 46:10 to, *"Be still, and know that I am God."* Countless number of Christians have their spiritual mailbox overflowing, but they are going around wondering why God is not speaking to them. If you have been connecting with God correctly and you still do not know what He is saying to you, most likely, you have not been practicing being still to hear from Him.

Your Passion

God's vision for our lives can also be communicated to us indirectly through our godly passion.

I am reminded of Nehemiah's story. It is never recorded in Scriptures that God spoke to Nehemiah to rebuild Jerusalem or that God sent a prophet to instruct Nehemiah to rebuild the walls of Jerusalem. He discovered this vision for his life through his godly passion.

Some Christians will never directly hear from God concerning His vision for their lives. This does not mean that your destiny is not important to God. No! It simply means that God is confident that He has put enough clues in your way to help you figure it out. This was Nehemiah's case.

He was comfortably serving King Artaxerxes as a cupbearer. By all standards, Nehemiah had a comfortable career. When Hanani visited him with some men from Judah and gave the report on the state of Jerusalem, he sat down and wept and mourned for many days, fasting and praying (Nehemiah 1:1-11). This is the true picture of passion. When you are truly passionate about something, its passion will drive you. Many of what we call passion today is simply a desire. Real passion made Nehemiah weep; real passion made Nehemiah fast and pray for many days. Real passion is not something that can be hidden. It will always be visible for all to see.

The mistake some passionate believers make is that they immediately begin going in the direction of their godly passion without taking it to God first. Nehemiah acknowledged in Nehemiah 2:18 that he made progress in the vision to rebuild Jerusalem because of *"the hand of God which had been good upon him, and also of the king's words that he had spoken to him."*

I see many believers erroneously start a Church simply because they love God and want to serve Him. They are so passionate about the things of God that they go ahead of themselves to start a Church and expect God to bless it. No matter how patriotic a citizen is, it will be considered a felony, or even worse, if they open an embassy for their country without being appointed ambassador by the President. Regardless of your passion, allow God to lead the way. Remember the words of Proverbs 16:3, *"Commit your works to the Lord, and your thoughts will be established."* Once you have discovered your area of passion, take it to God in prayer for confirmation before you match ahead. That you are passionate about a godly idea, does not mean you have been called/ordained to undertake it. David was passionate about building the temple of God, but God did not authorize him to do it, because his hands were soiled with blood (1 Chronicles 28:3). We will discuss how to confirm the vision you have gotten in a later chapter.

Seeking Him in Prayer

Prayer is the link that connects man to the throne room of God. If you must know the will of God in any situation, you must pray and ask Him. He promised to answer our prayers (Matthew 7:7). In fact, God said, *"Call to Me, and I will answer you, and show you great and mighty things, which you do not know"* (Jeremiah 33:3). Calling to God means to pray. It means connecting with God for communication.

Many believers are used to praying only the kind of prayers that get God to do something for them. We must learn to pray prayers of inquiry. In this kind of prayer, we ask God questions and wait for a response.

After David and his men lost their family and properties to invaders, in 1 Samuel 30, we see David praying a prayer of inquiry. He was not asking

God to fix everything for them; he asked God for what to do. In verse 8, David asks God, *"Shall I pursue this troop? Shall I overtake them?"* And He answered him, *"Pursue, for you shall surely overtake them and without fail recover all."* The kind of prayer that will cause God to reveal His vision for your life, is one of asking questions and expecting an answer. Proverbs 16:1 says, *"The preparations of the heart belong to man, but the answer of the tongue is from the Lord."*

Many believers question God's willingness to respond to their legitimate queries. Indeed, God does not answer every kind of question, but the Bible clearly tells us that God answers prayers that are prayed according to His will.

"Now this is the confidence that we have in Him, that if we ask anything according to His will, He hears us. And if we know that He hears us, whatever we ask, we know that we have the petitions that we have asked of Him." (1 John 5:14-15)

The next question is, *"Is it God's will to tell me His vision for my life?"* The answer is yes! God told the children of Israel, *"Ask Me of things to come concerning My sons; and concerning the work of My hands, you command Me."* (Isaiah 45:11)

Again, we are given another bold assurance concerning asking God. Amazingly, the Bible boldly says that everyone who asks receives. Meditate on this Scripture until it becomes a reality in your heart. Never give up asking from God because you seem not to have received it. Keep asking until your answer is received.

"Ask, and it will be given to you; seek, and you will find; knock, and it will be opened to you. For everyone who asks receives, and he who seeks finds, and to him who knocks it will be opened. Or what man is there among you who, if his son asks for bread, will give him a stone? Or if he asks for a fish, will he give him a serpent? If you then, being evil, know how to give good gifts to your children, how much more will your Father who is in heaven give good things to those who ask Him! Therefore, whatever you want men to do to you, do also to them, for this is the Law and the Prophets." (Matthew 7:7-12)

A note of caution is that you should never specify to God how you want Him to answer you. For instance, some people tell God to specifically respond to them through a dream, vision, or audible voice. Our job is to ask, and He promises that He will answer. It is God's prerogative to choose how your answer will be delivered.

God sees it as a sign of pride when we don't seek Him in prayer concerning decisions about our lives. Seeking God in prayer is not a suggestion; it is an expectation that God has of His children.

"For the shepherds have become dull-hearted, and have not sought the Lord; therefore they shall not prosper, and all their flocks shall be scattered." (Jeremiah 10:21)

"I will stretch out My hand against Judah, and against all the inhabitants of Jerusalem. I will cut off every trace of Baal from this place, the names of the idolatrous priests with the pagan priests—those who worship the host of heaven on the housetops; those who worship and swear oaths by the Lord, but who also swear by Milcom; those who have turned back from following the Lord, and have not sought the Lord, nor inquired of Him." (Zephaniah 1:4-6)

Begin to confidently talk to God in prayer concerning His plan for your life. He has never failed and will never fail (Zephaniah 3:5). He is the same yesterday, today and forever (Hebrews 13:8).

Spiritual Sensitivity

When you are in your home, expecting special guests, you make sure that you pay attention to the door. No matter what you do, your attention is fixed on the doorbell. The same goes if you expect a special phone call, email or message; your attention is fixed on your device. This same principle applies when we are expecting an answer from God. Habakkuk said, *"I will stand my watch And set myself on the rampart, And watch to see what He will say to me, And what I will answer when I am corrected."* (Habakkuk 2:1)

Many times, God speaks to us, but we are not sensitive enough to hear His voice. According to Scriptures, God sometimes speaks with a still, small voice (1 Kings 19:11-13). Elijah was not fooled by the strong wind, earthquake, and fire. The still small voice Elijah responded to, is what caused him to carry on the conversation with God.

Catching your vision from God requires sensitivity. God does not always respond to us while we are praying. God can decide to speak at any time of the day, and you must be attentive to His voice or leading when it comes. God can choose to speak to you as you are about to sleep (1 Samuel 3:1-10). If you value your sleep more than a conversation with God, you will miss out. Like Moses, God can choose to carry on a conversation with you for days (Exodus 34:27-28).

Spiritual sensitivity is cultivated as we learn to always be in an atmosphere filled with the fruit of the Holy Spirit. Anything contrary to the fruit of the Holy Spirit is capable of hindering your connection with God. Habits like worrying, complaining, nagging, negative thinking, etc. will hinder your sensitivity to God's voice. I speak peace in your soul and spirit in Jesus' mighty name!

Rise Up Early

We mentioned earlier that God sometimes speaks in a still small voice. As a result, it is a good practice to separate yourself to fellowship with God in a quiet environment. God speaks during the day and reveals knowledge during the night (Psalms 19:2).

Spending time with God late at night or in the early hours of the day, i.e. before dawn, affords you the quietness and stillness to hear from God. This is because you have not yet been hemmed in by the activities of the day. Depending on your level of spiritual growth, it is sometimes difficult to hear from God in the busyness of the day. Deliberately spending time with God early in the morning or the middle of the night allows you to focus on Him in stillness, to hear His word and see what He is saying to you clearly.

When you wake up in the middle of the night, you can spend time worshipping Him, praying in the Spirit or even reading the Word of God. After some time, simply say something along the lines of, *"Father, I am here to fellowship with you; please speak to me."* Now, simply be quiet and wait for His word to come through. You can stop praying or singing so you can clearly hear Him. Inasmuch as God does speak to us while we are worshipping, praying, etc., it is sometimes more beneficial to be quiet to hear him. You might see a picture, a word, etc., engage with it in faith and allow God to speak to you. In the beginning, this might be difficult as you may not be sure if the voice you hear is God's, the devil's or yours. Don't give up; persist in it and it will become easier for you to discern the difference. We will discuss how to distinguish God's voice from other voices in another chapter.

Separate Yourself

You need to be correctly positioned to see what God is showing you and to catch His vision for your life. It is not always possible to hear God everywhere. Sometimes, we need to physically separate ourselves in order to focus on God. God called Moses to separate himself by coming up the mountain. It ended up being a forty-day encounter.

In Revelations 4:1, Apostle John was told, *"Come up here, and I will show you things which must take place after this."* There is a time of separation to clearly hear from God. This is expedient during times when a few hours in the middle of the night will not be enough. From scriptural examples, we see that God can request our attention (Revelation 4:1, Exodus 34:27-28), or we can choose to separate ourselves to seek God's face (Galatians 1:7, Genesis 32:22-24).

In 2012, God told me to find a quiet place so He could speak to me. I lodged in a hotel for three days, and it was there that some portion of the vision that God gave me for the ministry was delivered. The separation does not have to be in a physical mountain like Moses; it can be anywhere we can focus squarely on God without distraction. From this experience, God instructed me to separate myself to seek His face at least once every quarter.

You must be willing to pay the price of separation to access His glorious vision for your life. You will never lose out if you separate yourself to seek God!

4

A Vision of Your New Identity

One critical kind of vision every triumphant believer must catch is the vision of their new identity in Christ.

Since time immemorial, man has been asking the question, "Who Am I?" This question is loaded with a need for self-discovery, understanding, a higher purpose, and inner peace.

Did I evolve from apes as is postulated by some? Was I created by the Most High God? These are questions that border around the vision we have of our identity. From the beginning of time, people have been asking those questions. Your answers to those questions will determine the height you will attain in life and your walk with God. It is written that *"The people who know their God shall be strong, and carry out great exploits."* (Daniel 11:32)

Without faith, it is impossible to grasp a revelation of things we cannot see naturally. It takes faith to discover who you are and continually walk in light of that truth.

A truth is information that proceeds from God. It is sometimes not verifiable by man-made means but is true regardless. On the other hand, a fact is made up of information that can be verified by man-made means. Sometimes, truth and fact are the same; at other times, they are at loggerheads. We will be examining some biblical truths about who we are in Christ. Receive them by faith, and you will be empowered to become them.

One of the most insightful declarations made by Jesus Christ is what we call the *"I AM Statements."* The gospels contain them.

I AM the Bread of Life

And Jesus said to them, "I am the bread of life. He who comes to Me shall never hunger, and he who believes in Me shall never thirst." (John 6:35)

"I am the bread of life." (John 6:48)

I AM the Way the Truth and the Life

Jesus said to him, "I am the way, the truth, and the life. No one comes to the Father except through Me." (John 14:6)

I AM the Light of the World

Then Jesus spoke to them again, saying, "I am the light of the world. He who follows Me shall not walk in darkness, but have the light of life." (John 8:12)

"As long as I am in the world, I am the light of the world." (John 9:5)

I AM the Door

"I am the door. If anyone enters by Me, he will be saved, and will go in and out and find pasture." (John 10:9)

I AM the Good Shepherd

"I am the good shepherd. The good shepherd gives His life for the sheep." (John 10:11)

I AM the Resurrection and the Life

Jesus said to her, "I am the resurrection and the life. He who believes in Me, though he may die, he shall live." (John 11:25)

I AM the True Vine

"I am the true vine, and My Father is the vinedresser." (John 15:1)

Before Abraham was, I AM

Jesus said to them, "Most assuredly, I say to you, before Abraham was, I AM." (John 8:58)

From these scriptural references, you see that Jesus showed us it is biblical to know who we are, declare who we are, and walk in the light of who we are.

Note that, even though Jesus knew who He was, it did not make Him become prideful. He knew what the devil fell into (i.e. pride) and avoided it at all costs.

"Let this mind be in you which was also in Christ Jesus, who, being in the form of God, did not consider it robbery to be equal with God, but made Himself of no reputation, taking the form of a bondservant, and coming in the likeness of men. And being found in appearance as a man, He humbled Himself and became obedient to the point of death, even the death of the cross. Therefore God also has highly exalted Him and given Him the name which is above every name, that at the name of Jesus every knee should bow, of those in heaven, and of those on earth, and of those under the earth, and that every tongue should confess that Jesus Christ is Lord, to the glory of God the Father."
(Philippians 2:5-11)

Now, let us examine who we are. As we explore them, may God open your eyes to catch a vision of your identity in Christ. They are a born-again Christian's *"I AM Statements."*

I am a Child of God

The child of a dog is a dog; the child of a bird is a bird; the child of God is a god.

- *"For as many as are led by the Spirit of God, these are sons of God. For you did not receive the spirit of bondage again to fear, but you received the Spirit of adoption by whom we cry out, "Abba, Father." The Spirit Himself bears witness with our spirit that we are children of God."* (Romans 8:14-16)

- *"For the earnest expectation of the creation eagerly waits for the revealing of the sons of God."* (Romans 8:19)

- *"For whom He foreknew, He also predestined to be conformed to the image of His Son, that He might be the firstborn among many brethren."* (Romans 8:29)

- *"But as many as received Him, to them He gave the right to become children of God, to those who believe in His name: who were born, not of blood, nor of the will of the flesh, nor of the will of man, but of God."* (John 1:12-13)

- *Jesus answered them, "Is it not written in your law, 'I said, 'You are gods'? If He called them gods, to whom the Word of God came (and the Scripture cannot be broken), do you say of Him whom the Father sanctified and sent into the world, 'You are blaspheming,' because I said, 'I am the Son of God?'"* (John 10:34-36)

- *"For you are all sons of God through faith in Christ Jesus."* (Galatians 3:26)

I am Complete in Christ

Every child of God has been made complete in Jesus Christ.

- *"Beware lest anyone cheat you through philosophy and empty deceit, according to the tradition of men, according to the basic principles of the world, and not according to Christ. For in Him dwells all the fullness of the Godhead bodily; and you are complete in Him, who is the head of all principality and power."* (Colossians 2:8-10)

- *"But God, who is rich in mercy, because of His great love with which He loved us, even when we were dead in trespasses, made us alive together with Christ (by grace you have been saved), and raised us up together, and made us sit together in the heavenly places in Christ Jesus."* (Ephesians 2:4-6)

- *"Love has been perfected among us in this: that we may have boldness in the day of judgment; because as He is, so are we in this world."* (1 John 4:17)

I am Co-Heir with Christ

A co-heir is one who is jointly inheriting the estate of the deceased. Even though God did not and cannot die, Jesus died so believers could have access to the divine inheritances that Adam lost when he sinned against God. We have joined Jesus Christ in laying claim to an inheritance in God.

- *"The Spirit Himself bears witness with our spirit that we are children of God, and if children, then heirs—heirs of God and joint heirs with Christ, if indeed we suffer with Him, that we may also be glorified together."* (Romans 8:16-17)

- *"And because you are sons, God has sent forth the Spirit of His Son into your hearts, crying out, "Abba, Father!" Therefore you are no longer a slave but a son, and if a son, then an heir of God through Christ."* (Galatians 4:6-7)

- *"And if you are Christ's, then you are Abraham's seed, and heirs according to the promise."* (Galatians 3:29)

I am Born to Win

As a child of God, losing is not in your DNA. God never loses a war. He commands the hosts of heaven and can engage seen and unseen forces to fight His battles. Likewise, we are not meant to lose. Failure is unbecoming of a child of God. Just like a lion births a lion, and the lion cub roars like its parents, a child of God is born to win like their Father in heaven.

- *"For whatever is born of God overcomes the world. And this is the victory that has overcome the world—our faith. Who is he who overcomes the world, but he who believes that Jesus is the Son of God?"* (1 John 5:4-5)

- *"But thanks be to God, who gives us the victory through our Lord Jesus Christ."* (1 Corinthians 15:57)

- *"He who comes from above is above all; he who is of the earth is earthly and speaks of the earth. He who comes from heaven is above all."* (John 3:31)

- *"No weapon formed against you shall prosper, and every tongue which rises against you in judgment you shall condemn. This is the heritage of the servants of the Lord, and their righteousness is from Me, says the Lord."* (Isaiah 54:17)

I am a New Creation

Immediately, I became a born-again Christian, and a radical transformation took place in the spiritual realm. My inherent nature changed.

When you become born again, you are recreated to the way Adam was in the Garden of Eden; entirely back in the image of God, with all the glory and authority that comes with it.

- *"Therefore, if anyone is in Christ, he is a new creation; old things have passed away; behold, all things have become new." (2 Corinthians 5:17)*

- *"What shall we say then? Shall we continue in sin that grace may abound? Certainly not! How shall we who died to sin live any longer in it? Or do you not know that as many of us as were baptized into Christ Jesus were baptized into His death? Therefore we were buried with Him through baptism into death, that just as Christ was raised from the dead by the glory of the Father, even so we also should walk in newness of life. For if we have been united together in the likeness of His death, certainly we also shall be in the likeness of His resurrection, knowing this, that our old man was crucified with Him, that the body of sin might be done away with, that we should no longer be slaves of sin. For he who has died has been freed from sin. Now if we died with Christ, we believe that we shall also live with Him, knowing that Christ, having been raised from the dead, dies no more. Death no longer has dominion over Him. For the death that He died, He died to sin once for all; but the life that He lives, He lives to God." (Romans 6:1-10)*

I am Chosen

Every child of God has been chosen for good works. We do not need to struggle to be accepted or seek validation from another human. God has a place for every believer in the body of Christ.

- *"But you are a chosen generation, a royal priesthood, a holy nation, His own special people, that you may proclaim the praises of Him who called you out of darkness into His marvelous light; who once were not a people but are now the people of God, who had not obtained mercy but now have obtained mercy."* (1 Peter 2:9-10)

- *"For you are a holy people to the LORD your God; the LORD your God has chosen you to be a people for Himself, a special treasure above all the peoples on the face of the earth."* (Deuteronomy 7:6)

- *Looking for the blessed hope and glorious appearing of our great God and Savior Jesus Christ, who gave Himself for us, that He might redeem us from every lawless deed and purify for Himself His own special people, zealous for good works.* (Titus 2:13-14)

I am a King and Priest

Every born-again Christian has been redeemed by God to reign on the earth, either as a King or Priest. This means our place of leadership is either in the secular world or the body of Christ. They are equally glorious callings. Not all born-again Christians are called by God to be Priests.

- *"And hath made us kings and priests unto God and his Father; to him be glory and dominion forever and ever. Amen."* (Revelation 1:6)

- *"And hast made us unto our God kings and priests: and we shall reign on the earth."* (Revelation 5:10)

I am the Light of the World

Every child of God is redeemed to shine the light of Jesus Christ in a dark world. We must be an example to others in our words, conduct, love, spirit, faith, and purity.

- *"You are the light of the world. A city that is set on a hill cannot be hidden. Nor do they light a lamp and put it under a basket, but on a lampstand, and it gives light to all who are in the house. Let your light so shine before men, that they may see your good works and glorify your Father in heaven."* (Matthew 5:14-16)

- *"Then Jesus spoke to them again, saying, "I am the light of the world. He who follows Me shall not walk in darkness, but have the light of life."* (John 8:12)

I am the Salt of the Earth

Salt acts as a preservative and enhances the taste of food. Every believer is to preserve Godliness wherever they are placed by God and to beautify wherever they are placed by God.

- *"You are the salt of the earth; but if the salt loses its flavor, how shall it be seasoned? It is then good for nothing but to be thrown out and trampled underfoot by men."* (Matthew 5:13)

These and many more, are the *"I Am Statements"* in the Bible that paint a picture of who we are redeemed to be. If you are not operating in these truths, start by meditating on them until you believe and become the truths declared in these Scriptures.

Our Lord Jesus has accomplished all these for you, making them yours legally. If you only stop at the legal possession without entering it, you will never get it. You will only have them credited into your account, but you will never enjoy them; hence, the devil will take advantage of you. However, you can enter into them through faith in the finished work of Christ. God has designed faith as a basic requirement you must have and exercise, to get anything from Him. God Himself said, *"But without faith it is impossible to please him: for He that cometh to God must believe that He is, and that He is a rewarder of them that diligently seek Him."* (Hebrews 11:6)

Your faith must please God, for you to enter into your victory.

5

Confirm the Vision

THE IMPORTANCE OF CONFIRMING THE VISION

Not every vision we receive originates from God. Some visions are a reflection of the state of our hearts, while others are simply from the devil. According to Proverbs 14:12, *"There is a way that seems right to a man, but its end is the way of death."*

If you have no doubts about the origin of the vision you received, there is no need to go through the charade of seeking confirmation. However, if you have reason to doubt what you received, it is wisdom to pause and validate the vision, rather than sheepishly running with the vision. This can cause double-mindedness and an absence of peace.

We are encouraged by Scriptures to test all spiritual things; this is mainly because not all spiritual experiences originate from God. We are told in 1 Thessalonians 5:20-21, *"Do not despise prophecies. Test all things; hold fast what is good."*

Do not put confidence in your flesh (Philippians 3:3). Claiming that you can never be deceived, already shows that deception has taken hold of you. If the devil could deceive one-third of the angels of God (Revelation 12:4), we will do well to take heed lest we fall. The devil is also known to manifest as an angel of light (2 Corinthians 11:14), but he is not an angel of light.

A vision that is not from God might flourish for a while, but sudden failure and destruction is inevitable. Before you start running with a vision, vet it to ensure it is from God.

As mentioned above, a vision can originate from the visionary themselves, either knowingly or unknowingly. When a person falls into the trap of covetousness, jealousy, envy, unforgiveness or bitterness, they are exposed to the devil's deception. These vices take place in a person's heart, which can affect their ability to discern what is truly from God. This is dangerous because you can begin to experience voices and/ or visions from within you that might not necessarily be from the Holy Spirit. That is why the Bible advises us to, *"Keep our heart with all diligence, for out of it spring the issues of life."* (Proverbs 4:23) We are also instructed in Ephesians 5:17, *"Therefore do not be unwise, but understand what the will of the Lord is."*

There is a spiritual principle that should be noted at this juncture. In the spiritual realm, the devil and his demons cannot intercept prayers properly addressed to God. In Jeremiah 33:3, the Bible says, *"Call on Me and I will answer."* It did not say *"Call on Me and the devil might answer you before I do."* It is important to note that if we direct our prayers to God, only God will answer it. If you simply ask questions without mentioning who they are directed to, any spiritual influence in the atmosphere has the right to respond to you; such would instigate and/or cause confusion. For example, there is a significant difference between saying, *"Holy Spirit, how should I handle this situation?"* versus, *"How should I handle this situation?"* When you properly direct your prayers to our Heavenly Father, you should not be afraid that you might receive a counterfeit answer.

How Do You Know the Vision is Confirmed?

The Peace of God

Anything that originates from God carries the fruit of the Holy Spirit with it. The fruit of particular importance here is peace. Peace is the state of rest we experience internally, regardless of what is happening externally. Jesus Christ said, *"Peace I leave with you, My peace I give to you; not as the world gives do I give to you. Let not your heart be troubled, neither let it be afraid."* (John 14:27)

Be sensitive to the presence or absence of the peace of God in your heart, when thinking about the vision you received. The lack of peace will make you unsettled; this is different from being fearful. The lack of peace will make it seem like, something is missing but you cannot place your finger on it.

"Let the peace of Christ [the inner calm of one who walks daily with Him] be the controlling factor in your hearts [deciding and settling questions that arise]. To this peace indeed you were called as members in one body [of believers]. And be thankful [to God always]." (Colossians 3:15, AMP)

In line with Scripture

There are many stories of people who have gotten so-called visions, purportedly originating from God, which was truly not the case. God will never contradict Himself. Whatever He reveals to us will be in agreement with the Scriptures, either in principle or directly.

For example, a woman supposedly receives a word from God that another woman's husband was hers, and since, *"The kingdom of heaven suffers violence, and the violent take it by force"* (Matthew 11:12), she proceeds to contend with the other woman to take her husband.

While this sounds scriptural, it is completely out of agreement with the Bible. A house divided against itself will fall (Matthew 12:25); God will never speak what violates the integrity of His word. This was definitely not from God, since it contradicted His word in Mark 10:9, *"For this reason a man shall leave his father and mother and be joined to his wife, and the two shall become one flesh'; so then they are no longer two, but one flesh. Therefore what God has joined together, let not man separate."*

When confirming visions using Scriptures, remember that even the devil has knowledge of Scriptures. The woman in the earlier example was misguided because she took Matthew 11:12 out of its context and twisted it to confirm the malicious word she received. The Scripture references we use to confirm or reject visions must be contextualized.

God's word is the surest tool for testing every vision that is received to ensure its validity.

I remember an incident that took place while I was praying in Toronto. I heard a voice quote a Scripture to me. Immediately I read that Scripture, the voice said that I am the messiah to come. This can sound great to some, but it was certainly a lie; immediately, I knew that voice was not of God. I was able to avoid deceit because I knew the voice I heard was saying something that was not in agreement with Scriptures.

The Bible speaks highly of a group of Jews in Berea.

"Then the brethren immediately sent Paul and Silas away by night to Berea. When they arrived, they went into the synagogue of the Jews. These were more fair-minded than those in Thessalonica, in that they received the word with all readiness, and searched the Scriptures daily to find out whether these things were so. Therefore many of them believed, and also not a few of the Greeks, prominent women as well as men." (Acts 17:10-12)

Before you start running with a vision you have received, subject it to biblical examination. When in doubt, seek insight from your Pastor or spiritual authority.

Prayer Confirmation

Children are taught in schools to ask questions when they don't understand. The same applies to us believers; we should learn to check with God in prayer. Sometimes, our confusion can be dispelled by simply saying, ***"Heavenly Father, I am not sure if this vision I received is from you. Please confirm to me if it is indeed from you. Thank you, Father, because I know you have heard and will answer me. Amen"***

God is not an author of confusion. In Jeremiah 29:12-13, He says *"Then you will call upon Me and go and pray to Me, and I will listen to you. And you will seek Me and find Me, when you search for Me with all your heart."*

Let us examine Gideon's example in confirming God's plan for his life. God sent an Angel to Gideon, to tell him that he was the chosen man to defeat Israel's oppressors. He doubted the word he heard and boldly asked for confirmation. This is recorded in Judges 6:17 (AMP), *"Gideon replied to Him, 'If I have found any favor in Your sight, then show me a sign that it is*

You who speaks with me.'" The Angel of God confirmed that the word was indeed from God.

A word of caution, though: We are not meant to always doubt what God is saying, thereby asking for confirmation for every word we receive. Asking God for confirmations must not take away our responsibility to act in faith. When in doubt, however, we should confidently ask God for clarification.

Another caution is that this should not be done in an atmosphere of unbelief or as a prerequisite for obedience. When these prayer confirmations are asked from a place of faith, belief, and a sincere heart, God always honours it.

Zechariah questioned the Angel of God from a place of unbelief and ended up dumb until the fulfilment of God's word (Luke 1:5-20). On the other hand, Mary questioned the angel of God from a place of faith and got more clarification, strengthening her faith (Luke 1:26-38).

Two or Three "Credible" Witnesses

A vision from God can also be confirmed by two or three credible witnesses. A witness is someone who experienced the same event. In most cases, your spiritual authority is a credible witness God has put in your life.

A person who is under spiritual authority can take advantage of this option. Whatever God says concerning your life has already been revealed in some manner to your true spiritual authority. We see this in the ministry of Jesus Christ. God the Father is Jesus Christ's spiritual authority, and He confirmed the visions and callings on His life in several instances. In one instance, when Jesus spoke with the Jews, He confirmed that John the Baptist and God the Father testified of Him.

"If I bear witness of Myself, My witness is not true. There is another who bears witness of Me, and I know that the witness which He witnesses of Me is true. You have sent to John, and he has borne witness to the truth. Yet I do not receive testimony from man, but I say these things that you may be saved. He was the burning and shining lamp, and you were willing for a time to rejoice in his light. But I have a greater witness than John's; for the works which the Father has given Me to finish—the very works that I do—bear witness of Me, that the Father has sent Me. And the Father Himself, who sent Me, has testified of Me. You have neither heard His voice at any time, nor seen His form. But you do not have His word abiding in you, because whom He sent, Him you do not believe. You search the Scriptures, for in them you think you have eternal life; and these are they which testify of Me. But you are not willing to come to Me that you may have life." (John 5:31-40)

The birth of Jesus Christ was confirmed by many credible witnesses in the Old and New Testament, from Isaiah to Micah and Malachi. Even in the New Testament, the birth of Christ was revealed to Anna the Prophetess and Simeon (Luke 2:25-38).

If you find yourself in a position where you are the only one who sees the vision God has given to you, and your genuine spiritual authorities have no inclination of that, please seek God to confirm it. Never take the absence of a confirmation from your spiritual authority lightly. It is part of the protection God has put in place for your destiny.

Identify the Personality

The voice of a person carries their personality with it. A fearful person will display fear in their speech; a confident person will speak confidently; a person who has faith will speak words of faith; a person who lacks faith will speak words of unbelief; a person who is not honest or straightforward will speak ambiguously, and so forth. The same goes for spiritual forces. Every voice from the spiritual realm carries the personality of the force behind it.

One of the ways to confirm a vision is by identifying the personality behind the message you are receiving concerning your vision. For example, if the vision you received includes spiteful comments about someone else, most likely that is not from God. A voice that says, *"My daughter, I have called you for a time as this. I am calling you to build me a Church for the next generation. This Church will be greater and better than denomination X's Church. I the lord have spoken."* You can see from this message that it is meant to breed selfish ambition and competition. It also goes against the Scripture that says, *"For where envy and self-seeking exist, confusion and every evil thing are there."* (James 3:16)

By discerning the personality of the voice speaking to us, we can tell whether it is the voice of God, the voice of the devil, or even our own voice.

A little while after Cornerstone Christian Church of God was started according to the will of God, I heard a gentle voice say to me while I was praying, *"Go back to your former Church. I have not called you to start a Church movement."* This baffled me, but I kept quiet to hear more so I could rightly test the spirit behind the voice. As I was quiet, the voice intensified and became violent; it even started cursing me and saying God did not call me. Immediately I heard this, I knew it was not the voice of

God, because it was not consistent with the personality and character of God.

Do not allow yourself to be intimidated by unclean spirits masquerading as the Spirit of God. Elijah experienced something similar when he went to meet with God. While he was waiting to hear from God, there was a strong wind, then an earthquake and finally fire, but God was not in it. Elijah could discern the voice of God; he knew that other signs did not carry the personality of God in them.

Beloved, there is nothing as refreshing as knowing that God has a plan for you. Nothing is as fulfilling as walking in that plan to manifest your enviable future.

"For I know the thoughts that I think toward you, says the LORD, thoughts of peace and not of evil, to give you a future and a hope." (Jeremiah 29:11)

Remember the instruction and promise we were given in Philippians 4:6-7, *"Be anxious for nothing, but in everything by prayer and supplication, with thanksgiving, let your requests be made known to God; and the peace of God, which surpasses all understanding, will guard your hearts and minds through Christ Jesus."*

May the peace of God go with you, as you seek Him to know His will for your life. May God grant you the wisdom to confirm the vision you have received.

6

Execute the Vision

Nothing is as frustrating as knowing where you are going but not knowing how to get there. In fact, the Bible calls this foolishness. It says in Ecclesiastes 10:15, *"The labor of fools wearies them, for they don't even know how to go to the city!"*

Having a glorious vision but not executing it properly is akin to foolishness. In this chapter, we will discuss some of the steps to take to ensure the fulfillment of the glorious destiny God has for us.

HOW TO EXECUTE THE VISION

Initial Stealth Mode

Immediately, God shows you His plan for your life, you are meant to leave it in the incubator of your heart. Avoid the mistake of quickly announcing the vision to everyone. If you share the vision with others prematurely, there is a high risk the vision will suffer a miscarriage. When you share the vision without understanding it yourself, there is a high risk that it will be miscarried. One of the main takeaways from this stage is to understand your "why." Once you connect with why God's vision must be accomplished, you will be more resilient and indefatigable.

No one understands everything God is saying by thinking about it once. God's ways are higher than our ways, and His thoughts than our thoughts (Isaiah 55:8-9). It takes some time of constant meditation and the help of the Holy Spirit to understand what God is saying. It is like a sixty-year-old person sharing deep things with a two-year-old child.

The initial stealth mode is for you to keep the vision to yourself so that you can understand the ramifications and ask relevant questions to aid your understanding. Nehemiah did the same. It was not until Nehemiah 2:3 that he revealed the vision to the king and his wife. We read in subsequent verses that, by the time he shared the vision with the king and his wife (i.e. spiritual authority), he already had details of what he would need to fulfill his vision.

Once you discover God's vision for your life, many forces are ready to contend with you. They are waiting for the announcement, and you need to be strong enough before the battle begins.

Some people get a vision to start a business empire from God. Straightaway, they share it with their spouse, friends and family. Let me mention here that, sometimes, visions are not aborted because of the evil intentions in people; at times, it is done unknowingly. Immediately, friends and family hear the vision you received, and they are excited and begin to ask relevant and valid questions; they usually expect an answer from you. Without an acceptable answer, you can become discouraged, frustrated and even begin to doubt the vision.

If you take your time to get more clarity from God before you begin to share the vision with close friends, you will have more confidence and be ready to answer their questions. Granted, you will never have all the answers you need initially, but some key questions need to be answered to have clarity and confidence.

Apostle Paul did the same. He narrated this in Galatians 1:16-17, *"To reveal His Son in me, that I might preach Him among the Gentiles, I did not immediately confer with flesh and blood, nor did I go up to Jerusalem to those who were apostles before me; but I went to Arabia, and returned again to Damascus."*

When God began to speak to me about going into ministry, I asked Him many questions about the ministry before sharing the vision with anyone. Your vision and destiny are sacred. Treat your vision as something sacrosanct. Among other questions, I asked questions like: Was it in the ministry where I was serving or a new one? What is the name of the ministry going to be? What is the vision of the ministry? When should the ministry start? Where should the ministry kick-off? After answering these key questions, I was ready to share the vision with the right team.

The voice said, "Cry out!" And he said, "What shall I cry?" "All flesh is grass, And all its loveliness is like the flower of the field." (Isaiah 40:6)

Even when you have gotten an instruction from God, you are to spend time asking, *"what you should cry."* The vision should remain in the incubation stage until you get the answers to clarify the call.

Share the Vision

Once you have gotten sufficient answers to clarify the vision you have received, it is time to share it. When it is time to share the vision, are we to simply share it with every Tom, Dick, and Harry? The answer is no, not yet.

The vision has to be shared with the right team. That right team consists of three categories of people: **mentors (spiritual authority), colleagues (or business partners), and mentees (employees).**

Sharing the vision with the right team causes the dream to start gaining expression. If properly done, the vision is already on its way to becoming a reality. We see an example of this in Nehemiah's approach. After going through the initial stealth mode, Nehemiah shared the vision with King Artaxerxes and his wife, the Queen (spiritual authorities), and then with the elders in Judah (colleagues) before he shared it with those who will do the work (employees).

Mentor (Spiritual Authority)

Immediately, you are ready to share the vision, the first group of people that should hear it should be your spiritual authorities. These are people that God has put in authority over you. They can be your spiritual leader, parents, etc. If you cannot trust your spiritual authorities with the vision, they are not truly an authority over you. For more insight on determining your spiritual authorities, read the book I authored, *"The Blessings of Being Under Spiritual Authority."*

Your spiritual authorities will be able to help you further understand the vision you have received from God. In the case of Nehemiah, your mentors can even help provide the needed resources to get you started. Because Nehemiah went through the initial stealth mode, he could clearly answer the king and his wife's questions.

"And it came to pass in the month of Nisan, in the twentieth year of King Artaxerxes, when wine was before him, that I took the wine and gave it to the king. Now I had never been sad in his presence before. Therefore the king said to me, "Why is your face sad, since you are not sick? This is nothing but sorrow of heart." So I became dreadfully afraid, and said to the king, "May the king live forever! Why should my face not be sad, when the city, the place of my fathers' tombs, lies waste, and its gates are burned with fire?" Then the king said to me, "What do you request?" So I prayed to the God of heaven. And I said to the king, "If it pleases the king, and if your servant has found favor in your sight, I ask that you send me to Judah, to the city of my fathers' tombs, that I may rebuild it." Then the king said to me (the queen also sitting beside him), "How long will your journey be? And when will you return?" So it pleased the king to send me; and I set him a time. Furthermore I said to the king, "If it pleases the king, let letters be given to me for the governors of the region beyond the River, that they must permit me to pass through till I come to Judah, and a letter to Asaph the keeper of the king's forest, that he must give me timber to make beams for the gates of the citadel which pertains to the temple, or the city wall, and for the house that I will occupy." And the king granted them to me according to the good hand of my God upon me." (Nehemiah 2:1-8)

Another merit of sharing the vision with your mentors is that it provides accountability. The moment you receive the vision is usually the most exciting time. The challenges arise when you attempt to bring what you have seen in the vision to reality. During the execution of your vision, being accountable to the people you love and respect comes in handy. If you don't share your vision with your mentors, it'll be easy to give up when tough times arise.

It is quite unfortunate that many people receive visions from God, hide them from their spiritual authority, and sneakily implement them. If Nehemiah had done that, he would have suffered unnecessarily and would have even been unable to implement his vision. Remember, the assumption here is that you are under genuine spiritual authority. A true mentor will do all they can to help you fulfil your God-given vision.

When sharing your vision with your mentors, pay close attention to their comments, opinions and advice. Doing so will save you time and resources in the future. Ask your mentors questions, and ensure you intentionally seek their commitment to stand by you throughout the journey.

Colleagues

Once your mentors are aware of the vision, share it with those who will walk alongside you in fulfilling it. In the case of a business idea, this will be your spouse and prospective business partners. In the case of a ministry, it could be your spouse, etc.

After Nehemiah shared the vision with the King and his wife, he travelled to Judah to share it with his colleagues. He was planning to partner with them, requiring their commitment and dedication. Before he shared the vision with them though, he took time to assess the work that needed to be done.

"So I came to Jerusalem and was there three days. Then I arose in the night, I and a few men with me; I told no one what my God had put in my heart to do at Jerusalem; nor was there any animal with me, except the one on which I rode. And I went out by night through the Valley Gate to the Serpent Well and the Refuse Gate, and viewed the walls of Jerusalem which were broken down and its gates which were burned with fire. Then I went on to the Fountain Gate and to the King's Pool, but there was no room for the animal under me to pass. So I went up in the night by the valley, and viewed the wall; then I turned back and entered by the Valley Gate, and so returned. And the officials did not know where I had gone or what I had done; I had not yet told the Jews, the priests, the nobles, the officials, or the others who did the work." (Nehemiah 2:11-16)

To gain credibility with your partners, you need facts about the vision that will energize them. They need to know that you are aware of the problem, that you possess the resources to address it, and that you know what is required from them for the fulfillment of the vision.

Prayerfully choose your colleagues and ensure that they have the expertise to contribute to the success of the vision. Colleagues should not be selected simply based on sentimental reasons like family lineage or long-term friendship. Bringing the wrong people on the journey will surely kill the vision.

The partnership is strengthened when each partner knows the value they are adding to the fulfilment of the vision and is committed to doing what it will take to add that value.

Also, prayerfully select those people who share the virtues that will ensure the continued success and growth of the vision. They must exude the fruit of the Holy Spirit, have a relationship with God, be people of integrity and good character, be hardworking, and be people you can trust when the chips are down.

Mentee

The next category of people the vision should be shared with are your mentees. They are also those who will be doing the work. In many instances, the visioner is the leader and has to be responsible for making sure everyone is playing their role to see the vision actualized.

In the earthly ministry of Jesus Christ, He had his twelve disciples. They were carefully hand-picked after an all-night prayer session.

"Now it came to pass in those days that He went out to the mountain to pray, and continued all night in prayer to God. And when it was day, He called His disciples to Himself; and from them He chose twelve whom He also named apostles: Simon, whom He also named Peter, and Andrew his brother; James and John; Philip and Bartholomew; Matthew and Thomas; James the son of Alphaeus, and Simon called the Zealot; Judas the son of James, and Judas Iscariot who also became a traitor." (Luke 6:12-16)

This is also a very critical decision. A mistake in this stage can cripple the fulfilment of the vision. Jesus knew the importance of that decision, which is why He spent the whole night praying about it. Perhaps he got the names of the other Apostles pretty early in prayers, but he had to negotiate to add Judas Iscariot to the list the whole night.

The mentees should know what is expected of them. They should know the extent to which the vision is going. They should unequivocally know of your commitment to the vision and their success in it. They should be aware of your support throughout the actualization of the vision.

Remember, you will be accountable to God for the fulfilment of the vision He has given you. Please, *"Do not give what is holy to the dogs; nor cast your pearls before swine, lest they trample them under their feet, and turn and tear you in pieces."* (Matthew 7:6) That simply means, you should not share your valuable vision with people that will treat it with disgust.

7

Protect the Vision

Every genuine God-given vision will face internal and external attacks. Your knowledge of those attacks and a commitment to protecting your vision from them will ensure the longevity of your vision.

ATTACKS AGAINST THE VISION

External Attacks

Do not be naive; you will have enemies no matter how good your vision is. There will always be someone whose survival depends on the death of your vision. Your vision is an existential threat to them. Hence, they will bring the fight on, and you must be ready to defend your vision. These external attacks are designed to destroy your vision from the outside.

Suppose your vision is to end the scourge of illicit drugs in a neighbourhood. In that case, you must understand its implications, which are you indirectly going to war with those who have built their livelihood on the manufacturing, distribution and sale of those illicit drugs. If your vision is to stop child trafficking, understand that you are indirectly going to war with those whose livelihood depends on trafficking children. The vision God has given to you is worth defending.

Jesus Christ knew where external attacks would come from, and He faced them head-on. Never think that the enemies of your vision will become your friends. Be prepared to thrive despite the existence of those enemies. Be ready to do what it takes, within the confines of acceptable godly behaviour, to keep your enemies at bay and your vision alive and thriving.

Let us yet again refer to Nehemiah's story. Nehemiah never knew he had enemies until he located God's vision for his life. Don't take it personally; your enemies just hate you because of the vision you are pursuing. You have decided to love what they hate; you have decided to hate what they love. We see in Nehemiah 2:9-10: *"Then I went to the governors in the region beyond the River, and gave them the king's letters. Now the king had sent captains of the army and horsemen with me. When Sanballat the Horonite and Tobiah the Ammonite official heard of it, they were deeply disturbed that a man had come to seek the well-being of the children of Israel."*

You will do well to realize that the attacks against you are not personal. You are being attacked because you chose to obey God, by pursuing the vision He gave you. The adversaries of the Israelites made their intentions known in Nehemiah 4:11: *"And our adversaries said, 'hey will neither know nor see anything, till we come into their midst and kill them and cause the work to cease.'"* The goal of their attackers was for the work to cease.

External attacks can lead to the immediate or indirect halt of the work you are doing. The enemy can overpower you and cause the work you are doing to cease, or the enemy can orchestrate events that will culminate in your giving up so that the work can cease.

The Attack of Fear

One of the most potent external attacks comes from an arch-enemy called fear. Fear is the spiritual force that tries to keep you from reaching your goals.

It leverages many means to achieve its goal. Some of those means include intimidation, harassment and oppression.

Every time you want to embark on something worthwhile, fear will always challenge your resolve. There is no exception. Once you understand that, you will build your strength to defeat fear.

There are three key steps to defeating fear in your life, and this also applies to other aspects of spiritual warfare. They are as follows: recognize (not rationalize) the fear, rebuke the spirit of fear, and determine wise steps to take and follow through despite the fear.

There are three main tools for defeating fear: **power, love, and a sound mind.** According to 2 Peter 1:7, *"God has not given us a spirit of fear, but of power and of love and of a sound mind."* In essence, this verse of Scripture says that in place of fear, God gave us power, love, and a sound mind.

Let us examine strategies for defending your vision against external attacks so you can keep pressing on to the finish line.

Strategies for Defending Your Vision

Power

The first defence against fear is power. Power helps the carrier to remove obstacles.

Since fear is a force, it takes the force of power to defeat it. Power is simply the ability to get things done. God overcame the obstacles by power so the earth could be created. Likewise, a life free of fear that we desire must be enforced with power.

Treat fear like you would treat the devil if he appeared to you. When you see fear trying to stop you from doing the right thing, remember there is something valuable at the other end of the tunnel.

As a believer, remember Jesus said, *"Behold, I give you the authority to trample on serpents and scorpions, and over all the power of the enemy, and nothing shall by any means hurt you."* (Luke 10:19) Whenever fear is trying to stop you, boldly declare, ***"I have not been given the spirit of fear but of power, love and a sound mind. I rebuke you spirit of fear now, in Jesus' name."***

Love

The second defence against fear is love. This love is God's kind of love, that is, agape love.

Love has the power to defeat fear. 1 John 4:18 states that, *"There is no fear in love; but perfect love casts out fear, because fear involves torment. But he who fears has not been made perfect in love."* When you walk in perfect love, fear will be a thing of the past.

Have you ever seen a hen protecting its chicks from a human being? At that moment, the hen forgets it is no match for the human. As a result of the perfect love that the hen has for its chicks, it can face any kind of opposition.

Sound Mind

The third defence against fear is a sound mind.

A sound mind is one that can correctly receive, process, and store information. That also means a mind that is not clogged. One of the things that fear makes a person do is think irrationally. For example, a person afraid of cockroaches might think that a cockroach is powerful enough to inflict harm on them. However, a person with a sound mind will certainly know what is reasonable and what is outrageous.

A sound mind will make you realize there is no need to fear darkness. The truth is, any demonic force that is worth its weight in gold, should be able to attack a person when the light is turned on, just like they can when the lights are off. Hence, it is not sound thinking to reason that the devil can only attack when dark. I rebuke that fear you have of darkness in Jesus' name! A sound mind lets people know when they are crossing the line, in what they accept to be true.

A sound mind will help a believer understand that, as long as they are walking with God in holiness, there is nothing the devil can do against them. If the devil could not kill and destroy you when you were not committed to God, how much more now that you are making every genuine effort to draw closer to Him.

External Enemies

Friends of Your Enemies (The Moles)

While pursuing God's vision for your life, expect external attacks from people like Sanballat, Tobiah, Geshem and others (in Nehemiah's case). What you should also expect are people within your circle who are in alliance with your enemies. I call them the friends of your enemies.

One of the things you will notice as you run with the vision is that the devil will have his agents within your inner circle. From biblical precedent, it seems like God intentionally allows it to happen. This is not an indictment on your part. It does not mean that you failed. You, however, must know who they are, to protect your vision from them and eventually boot them out.

Jesus Christ, our Master, Lord, and Saviour, had moles within his inner circle. Apostle Paul had moles within his inner circle. Even God the Father had a mole (Lucifer) in heaven. Do not kid yourself; at every point in time, there will be moles within your team; watch out for them.

Those friends of your enemies are also your friends; sometimes they are even your family. The truth is that they usually truly support the vision and want to see it succeed. Their problem, however, is that they have divided loyalties. They love the vision, and they also love something else that the enemies are using to hold them captive. It could be money, family connections, power, etc.

Contrary to what is believed in many Christian circles, the devil is not omniscient, i.e. he does not know everything. What the devil has built up is a tightly controlled web of informants.

When I studied the book of Nehemiah, I was amazed at how quickly the enemies of the vision heard about Nehemiah's steps. What was even more shocking was that, sometimes, they heard of his moves before he made them.

- *"When Sanballat the Horonite and Tobiah the Ammonite official heard of it, they were deeply disturbed that a man had come to seek the well-being of the children of Israel."* (Nehemiah 2:10)

- *"But when Sanballat the Horonite, Tobiah the Ammonite official, and Geshem the Arab heard of it, they laughed at us and despised us, and said, "What is this thing that you are doing? Will you rebel against the king?"* (Nehemiah 2:19)

- *"But it so happened, when Sanballat heard that we were rebuilding the wall, that he was furious and very indignant, and mocked the Jews."* (Nehemiah 4:1)

- *"Now it happened when Sanballat, Tobiah, Geshem the Arab, and the rest of our enemies heard that I had rebuilt the wall, and that there were no breaks left in it (though at that time I had not hung the doors in the gates)."* (Nehemiah 6:1)

As I studied further, I realized who the mole was. There was a family that had deep ties with Sanballat, Tobiah, Geshem, and the other enemies of the vision. Even though this family partook in the re-building work, they had divided loyalties that could have destroyed or made the work ineffective if

Nehemiah had not identified and dealt with them. The mole was Eliashib, the high priest, and his family.

Are you shocked that the mole was the high priest? You should not be. The higher the authority the mole has in your organization, the more damage the mole can do. Interestingly, Eliashib was the first to rise up to rebuild the wall. In other words, he was the first person to accept Nehemiah's vision and join him in the rebuilding process. Those the enemy will use in attacking your vision will appear spiritual; they will appear committed; they will appear loyal. Appearances can fool a person, but by their fruits, you will know them (Matthew 7:16). This is all the more reason why the visioner needs discernment (or to pray for discernment), in choosing partners for the vision.

"Then Eliashib the high priest rose up with his brethren the priests and built the Sheep Gate; they consecrated it and hung its doors. They built as far as the Tower of the Hundred, and consecrated it, then as far as the Tower of Hananel." (Nehemiah 3:1)

The same Eliashib was deeply connected with Tobiah. He even gave him unfettered access to the temple of God.

"Now before this, Eliashib the priest, having authority over the storerooms of the house of our God, was allied with Tobiah. And he had prepared for him a large room, where previously they had stored the grain offerings, the frankincense, the articles, the tithes of grain, the new wine and oil, which were commanded to be given to the Levites and singers and gatekeepers, and the offerings for the priests. But during all this I was not in Jerusalem, for in the thirty-second year of Artaxerxes king of Babylon I had returned to the king. Then after certain days I obtained leave from the king, and I came to Jerusalem and discovered the evil that Eliashib had done for Tobiah, in

preparing a room for him in the courts of the house of God. And it grieved me bitterly; therefore I threw all the household goods of Tobiah out of the room. Then I commanded them to cleanse the rooms; and I brought back into them the articles of the house of God, with the grain offering and the frankincense." (Nehemiah 13:4-9)

We also see in Nehemiah 13:28 that Eliashib had family connections with Sanballat.

"And one of the sons of Joiada, the son of Eliashib the high priest, was a son-in-law of Sanballat the Horonite; therefore I drove him from me." (Nehemiah 13:28)

This is why the deeper a person gets to the vision God has given to you, the more they are required to be exclusive to you and the vision. The same principle applies to our relationship with God. Everyone God intends to reveal Himself to, must be exclusive to Him alone. This is the definition of holiness, consecration and sanctification. You are simply saying, *"God from today I am exclusively yours and yours alone."* Even God Himself said, *"For you shall worship no other god, for the Lord, whose name is Jealous, is a jealous God."* (Exodus 34:14)

Even in the human body, the closer a germ or virus gets to vital organs, the deadlier it will be. As the visionary, you are the vital organ in the actualization of the vision God has given to you. Ensure that your heart is guarded at all times. Be mindful of the suggestions you are given; they might undermine the vision God has given to you.

May God open your eyes to see those the enemy might have planted in your team to destroy your vision from within. May God give you wisdom to repel every attack against your vision successfully.

Temptations

When God establishes His plan, the only person who can effectively hinder that plan is you!

Romans 8:31 asks a critical question that we often respond to wrongly. It says, *"What then shall we say to these things? If God is for us, who can be against us?"* The correct answer to that question is us. When God is for us, we are the only ones who can be against ourselves. The devil knows this, which is why he tempts us to turn God against us.

When running with our God-given vision, we need to be aware of temptation traps set by the devil to destroy us.

Temptations might seem innocuous, but they are designed to distract us from God's plan for our lives.

A temptation may look attractive, but they are lethal. Ask yourself these questions: What if Joseph slept with Potiphar's wife? What if the three Hebrew boys bowed to the king's statue? What if Jesus turned the stone to bread, bowed down to the devil or jumped from the top of the temple?

Erroneously, many people only think of adultery or fornication when thinking about temptations. A temptation is anything designed to make you disobey God, either by doing what He says you should not do or by not doing what He commands you to do.

INTERNAL ATTACKS

There are other types of attacks against the vision that, even though they originated from outside, aim to cause you, the visionary, to stop working on the vision. I call them internal attacks. They can be more subtle but powerful nonetheless.

Internal attacks vary in their ability to kill a vision. This section will discuss a few of them.

Discouragement

Discouragement occurs when one does not have the will and desire to keep pursuing the vision. Sometimes, this comes when one is tired of pursuing the God-given vision. A discouraged person will begin to ask questions like, *"What's the essence of all this work we are doing?"*

Understand that everyone who runs gets tired, everyone who walks gets tired, and everyone who fights gets tired. They don't blame themselves for being tired; instead, they rest, recuperate, and get back on track.

Deferred hope discourages a person (Proverbs 13:12). Hopelessness will make you impotent because, without faith, it is impossible to please God. If God could raise Lazarus from the dead, He can do anything. Discouragement comes when you are not seeing adequate results or no results at all. It is a silent killer. A discouraged person will self-destruct. They are the ones that end up committing physical suicide, or what I call vision suicide.

The only potent panacea for dealing with discouragement is joy. Whatever you do, make sure you are connected to an endless supply of joy if you want to protect yourself and the vision from self-destruction. Prophet

Habakkuk went through a rough period, but he knew what to do about it. He did not initiate a pity party; rather, he rejoiced in the Lord.

"Though the fig tree may not blossom, nor fruit be on the vines; though the labor of the olive may fail, and the fields yield no food; though the flock may be cut off from the fold, and there be no herd in the stalls—yet I will rejoice in the Lord, I will joy in the God of my salvation. The Lord God is my strength; he will make my feet like deer's feet, And He will make me walk on my high hills." (Habakkuk 3:17-19)

The good news is that joy is a fruit of the Holy Spirit, and it is yours for the taking. For an endless supply of joy, make sure you form the habit of gratitude. Make it a habit to keep track of things you are thankful to God. A discouraged person might have some areas for celebration, but most times, they are trumped by the areas of challenges. Never allow the challenges you are going through to affect your ability to celebrate. Be careful whenever you refuse to celebrate because of challenges; discouragement is just around the corner.

In the mighty name of Jesus Christ, I declare that every root of discouragement in your life be uprooted now!

Disappointment

Disappointment occurs when your expectations are not fulfilled. Disappointment comes about as a result of having unrealistic expectations or wrong expectations.

Discouragement is a gradual killer, while disappointment is a forceful killer. Whereas discouragement is subtle, happens slowly, and can be missed; disappointment is an event, and depending on the scope, it can be deadly to the vision.

Watch out for disappointment as you work on the vision God has given you. Watch out for unrealistic expectations in the course of running with your vision. Make sure that your expectations are in line with what God has said. Only He is infallible and faithful. If He has promised it, it will never fail (Joshua 21:45). On the other hand, if the expectations were of your desire, there is a chance that some will fail, mainly because God has a different plan for your life.

When you put your entire trust in a human being that can fail, you are putting yourself at risk of being disappointed. Have expectations of people, but never put them in the same infallible class as God.

Pride

This is a state of mind in which you elevate yourself above others. When you exalt yourself above others, you begin to overestimate your abilities, which eventually leads to your destruction from within.

God takes the issue of pride very personally. His former angel, Lucifer (devil), became prideful and subsequently rebelled against Him. God has personally committed to fighting against prideful people. Proverbs 16:5 states, *"Everyone proud in heart is an abomination to the LORD; though they join forces, none will go unpunished."* It is also written in James 4:6 that, *"God opposes the proud but shows favor to the humble."*

As you implement the vision, you will enjoy success. As you enjoy those successes, ensure you remain humble in your heart. Remember that no matter how high you are, someone is higher than you.

A prideful person simply says that they have reached the pinnacle of success and are satisfied with themselves. On the other hand, a humble person says that they still have a long way to go and have not arrived yet.

Pride is a condition of the heart. It is sometimes not easily detectable. Sadly, many cultures rely only on outward manifestations, such as how a person walks, talks, etc., to detect pride. Even though those measures are sometimes valid, at other times, they are not. You will have to rely on the Holy Spirit to help you identify those areas where you need to humble yourself under God. A person who is not under anyone's authority is prideful. A person who does not pray to God each day is prideful. A person who cannot receive correction is prideful. A person who never sees their wrongdoing is prideful. A person who does not see the need to learn from others is prideful.

If you allow pride to take hold of you, your vision will be destroyed from within. God Himself will see to it that the vision is not actualized. If the vision must be actualized, God will replace you with someone who will continue in your stead. God replaced Saul with David because the former allowed pride into his heart. This will not be your portion in Jesus' name. Let us also learn from what happened to King Belshazzar; *"But when his heart was lifted up, and his spirit was hardened in pride, he was deposed from his kingly throne, and they took his glory from him."* (Daniel 5:20) Your glory will not be taken from you in Jesus' name.

Remain humble!

Envy / Jealousy

Envy and jealousy are twin vices. Where you find one, you will most likely see the other.

A visionary should guard their hearts to avoid comparing themselves with others. It is good to admire other people, but it is bad to compare yourself with them. It is good to celebrate what God is doing in the lives of others, but it is bad to compare that to what God is doing in your life. Envy/jealousy is a vision killer.

The Bible tells us, *"Where envy and self-seeking exist, confusion and every evil thing are there."* (James 3:16) If you don't watch out, envy and jealousy will destroy your God-given vision from within. Be watchful of your team members, especially in this area of envy and jealousy. As the vision progresses, team members will vie for positions of power and authority. Be mindful of the steps they can take to attain power and authority; correct them when things are done wrongly.

In Jesus Christ's earthly ministry, envy and jealousy tried to rear their ugly heads, but our Master wisely nipped them in the bud. There are three notable instances of envy and jealousy: one was among James, John, and their mother; another was among the disciples; and the last was between Peter and John.

James and John

In one instance, the mother of James and John made an unusual request to Christ. She must have been a politician, as she was already lobbying for lucrative positions for her sons in the kingdom of God.

Jesus was fully aware of the repercussions of that request on the cohesion of His team and immediately nipped it in the bud. However, even though Jesus took immediate action, the damage had already been done; the other disciples became offended by the actions of James, John, and their mother.

"Then the mother of Zebedee's sons came to Him with her sons, kneeling down and asking something from Him. And He said to her, "What do you wish?" She said to Him, "Grant that these two sons of mine may sit, one on Your right hand and the other on the left, in Your kingdom." But Jesus answered and said, "You do not know what you ask. Are you able to drink the cup that I am about to drink, and be baptized with the baptism that I am baptized with?" They said to Him, "We are able." So He said to them, "You will indeed drink My cup, and be baptized with the baptism that I am baptized with; but to sit on My right hand and on My left is not Mine to give, but it is for those for whom it is prepared by My Father." And when the ten heard it, they were greatly displeased with the two brothers. But Jesus called them to Himself and said, "You know that the rulers of the Gentiles lord it over them, and those who are great exercise authority over them. Yet it shall not be so among you; but whoever desires to become great among you, let him be your servant. And whoever desires to be first among you, let him be your slave—just as the Son of Man did not come to be served, but to serve, and to give His life a ransom for many." (Matthew 20:20-28)

It is unfortunate that many visions have been destroyed from within because the leader either ignored the plague of envy/jealousy or fostered it for short-term gain.

An atmosphere where a leader encourages envy and jealousy might experience short-term growth, and people might even be motivated to do more, but it will always be short-lived. In the long run, a crash is inevitable because envy/jealousy inhibits sustainable growth.

Who is the Greatest?

Another instance of envy/jealousy manifesting itself in the ministry of Jesus Christ happened after the disciples enjoyed success in ministry. They had just returned from an outreach and saw God do amazing things through them. As expected, the devil sprang into action, enticing them with the idea that one can be greater than the other.

"Then a dispute arose among them as to which of them would be greatest. And Jesus, perceiving the thought of their heart, took a little child and set him by Him, and said to them, "Whoever receives this little child in My name receives Me; and whoever receives Me receives Him who sent Me. For he who is least among you all will be great." (Luke 9:46-48)

As surely as night follows day, you can expect the devil to always tempt members of a team to compete with one another, especially after experiencing success.

Visionary, watch out for the scourge of envy/jealousy within your team!

Peter And John

The last example we will review happened immediately after Peter was restored back to fellowship with Jesus Christ.

Christ had just visited Peter and the other disciples, and Christ had to address the elephant in the room: What would happen to Peter? Is he still part of the team?

After enjoying a meal with His disciples, Jesus turned to Peter, reinstated him, and reaffirmed his Apostleship. However, before Peter could celebrate his restoration, the enemy struck again. Peter displayed envy and jealousy towards John. He asked Jesus in a derogatory manner, *"But Lord, what about this man?"* (John 21:21)

Jesus' answer is one that every visionary should take to heart. Envy and jealousy should not be tolerated within the team. In John 21:22, we are told Jesus' response to Peter: *"If I will that he remain till I come, what is that to you? You follow Me."*

In essence, Jesus told Peter to mind his own business, to focus on his assignment, and to work out his own salvation with fear and trembling.

8

Execution Boosters (The 7 P's)

Planning

Planning is the act of determining the right steps to take to achieve a vision. Planning is perhaps one activity many Christians don't think they need to engage in if they want to walk by faith. This is indeed far from the truth. Walking by faith does not mean flying blindly. Walking by faith simply means that you believe God to fill in the unknowns, in your plan to achieve His vision.

In speaking about planning, Jesus said in Luke 14:28-33, *"For which of you, intending to build a tower, does not sit down first and count the cost, whether he has enough to finish it— lest, after he has laid the foundation, and is not able to finish, all who see it begin to mock him, saying, 'This man began to build and was not able to finish'? Or what king, going to make war against another king, does not sit down first and consider whether he is able with ten thousand to meet him who comes against him with twenty thousand? Or else, while the other is still a great way off, he sends a delegation and asks conditions of peace. So likewise, whoever of you does not forsake all that he has cannot be My disciple."* It is not a sin to plan. Even when you are walking by faith, plan based on the information that you have.

The Plan: Approach + Timeline

After you get your vision from God, the next question you should seek to answer is, *"How should I go about implementing this vision?"* Even though God has given many people similar visions, they do not all have the same strategy to implement that vision. The vision is a picture of your destination, while the strategy/plan is the approach and timeline for reaching that destination.

Before you can plan the actualization of your vision, you must have an idea of the strategy for implementation. A strategy is simply your unique approach to implementing the vision. For example, many battles were fought in Scriptures, but not every battle was fought the same way. Regarding fighting battles, the vision is to win the battle, while the plan is how the enemies will be defeated, where the enemies will be defeated, what enemies will be defeated first, who will defeat which enemies, etc.

Leaving God to fulfil the vision, without you actively planning is in violation of Luke 14:28-33; it will always lead to blatant failure. There is a battle in Scripture that amazes me every time I read it. This always reminds me of the need to have an approach in implementing the vision, and that it is not enough for God to show you the vision; you must have a plan.

Eleven tribes of Israel went to war with the tribe of Benjamin. Even though God clearly told them to go ahead and fight against the Benjamites, they lost at the first two attempts. From this story, we see that they only asked God simple questions like: Who should go up first? Should we attack them? This was not their first rodeo and God already expected them to know that they needed more information; it is no surprise that they lost, in their first two battle attempts. It was not until they devised a plan after seeking God that they won the battle (Judges 20:12-48).

There are three main, Bible-proven ways to discover the plan for actualizing God's vision for your life.

God Delivers the Plan to Man

In this approach, God tells you how to implement a vision. God can also share the perfect timing for those steps.

God gave Abraham a glorious vision that he would be the father of many nations. God Himself told Abraham to leave his father's house and where to settle down.

In the same vein, God showed His plans to Jesus Christ. Christ later testified about this in John 5:19-20: *"Then Jesus answered and said to them, "Most assuredly, I say to you, the Son can do nothing of Himself, but what He sees the Father do; for whatever He does, the Son also does in like manner. For the Father loves the Son, and shows Him all things that He Himself does; and He will show Him greater works than these, that you may marvel."*

Our God is wonderful in counsel and excellent in guidance (Isaiah 28:29). He knows way better than you do how to fulfill that vision. Seek Him today and find out His unique approach and timeline for fulfilling the plan He gave to you.

Man Discovers the Plan from Man

In this approach, you discover the approach by examining the steps others in a similar situation took. There are many documented stories of saints, who took brilliant steps in actualizing God's vision. The Bible itself is full of approaches that we can emulate.

You get this information by reading biographies, random stories, and/or interviews with men and women who have broken frontiers in the field you are called into. You can read about their approach and take it to God for validation before implementing any of it.

For example, when there was a famine in the land, Abraham went to Egypt (Genesis 12:10). What did Isaac do when he experienced famine? He planned to go down to Egypt just like his father had done, until God stepped in to tell him otherwise (Genesis 26:2). It is good to read about others' brilliant steps and consider them when in similar situations, but we must ensure that we are open to God's direction.

In implementing a vision, at least thousands of decisions will be made. The reality is that we will not directly hear from God concerning all those decisions. In some cases, God will give clear direction; in others, He will leave that to us to figure out and validate it with His peace in our hearts. Elisha saw how Elijah parted the Jordan, and when it was his turn, he simply followed the same approach (2 Kings 2:8-14).

Seek God concerning His unique approach and timeline for implementing your vision, and educate yourself on the brilliant steps others with a similar vision took.

Man Discovers the Plan

Under this approach, you arrive at the plan by thinking about it. For the right approach, you might draw from your personal experiences or knowledge. Proverbs 16:9 states, *"A man's heart plans his way, but the Lord directs his steps."*

There are times when God leaves us to figure out how to approach ourselves based on the wisdom He has already given us.

Gideon was faced with a battle of a lifetime. God had trimmed down his army to a meagre three hundred men, from thirty-two thousand. God then appeared to him and said, *"Arise, go down against the camp, for I have delivered it into your hand. But if you are afraid to go down, go down to the camp with Purah your servant, and you shall hear what they say; and afterward your hands shall be strengthened to go down against the camp"* (Judges 7:9-11). This was good, but after Gideon heard the dream a soldier shared, he discovered that God had indeed delivered them into their hands; Gideon's faith was strengthened, and he sprung to action. The Bible never recorded that God told Gideon the plan to defeat the enemy.

"Then he divided the three hundred men into three companies, and he put a trumpet into every man's hand, with empty pitchers, and torches inside the pitchers. And he said to them, "Look at me and do likewise; watch, and when I come to the edge of the camp you shall do as I do: When I blow the trumpet, I and all who are with me, then you also blow the trumpets on every side of the whole camp, and say, 'The sword of the Lord and of Gideon!'" (Judges 7:16-18)

Do not be afraid to run with the idea you get in your heart. You will sometimes get the approach in ways some deem unspiritual. For example, you might stumble on a plan of action while eating, reading an article, or speaking to a friend, not necessarily while praying or reading the Bible. You might not have explicitly gotten it from God, but ensure you are sensitive to His leading. Ensure that God still has the prerogative to step in and redirect your steps whenever He wants to. God expects His children to seek His counsel (Jeremiah 10:21).

Pursuit

After diligently planning, the next step is to implement the plan. This is the pursuit stage; it can also be called the running stage. Planning is difficult on its own, but the pursuit is indeed where the rubber meets the road. Well-laid-out plans that are not implemented are akin to not roasting what you took in hunting (Proverbs 12:27). You have practiced and rehearsed, and now is the time for the actual race. Your success will depend on how well you do what you have said you will do, during your planning stage. Will you do less than you planned, exactly what you planned, or go above and beyond what you planned?

Diligence and Discipline

In pursuing a vision, diligence is one of your most prized assets. For you to be diligent, you have to be disciplined. You will not always be excited to do what you love doing. This statement is difficult for a beginner, but it is true nonetheless. When you receive your vision, it will be impossible to see yourself not being excited about it, but this will undoubtedly happen. At times when there is no excitement, discipline is what will keep you going. I recommend that you read the book I authored, *"A Disciplined Life."* It will help you see how to apply discipline to every aspect of your being (spirit, soul (i.e. emotions, will, intellect) and body) so that you can actualize God's vision.

You cannot pursue two rabbits at the very same time; you will catch neither of them. Be focused on your vision, especially when you begin to enjoy success. Once a person becomes successful, many other profitable venture offers will start rolling in from numerous places. Be disciplined enough to ensure you don't get distracted from the vision God has given you at each stage. The fact that you received new ideas does not mean it is time to implement them. When in doubt, always check with your boss in heaven and allow Him to direct your steps in all things.

Avoid Burnout

As the visionary, watch out for burnout!

Burnout is a state you reach when you are not able to go further. Some people even suffer a physical, emotional or mental breakdown. Anyone can fall into this trap if they are not careful. Those that are burnt out are more susceptible to the devil's attacks. Only God neither faints nor gets weary. We avoid burnout by learning how to keep our strength renewed, even as we diligently pursue the vision God has given to us.

"Have you not known? Have you not heard? The everlasting God, the LORD, The Creator of the ends of the earth, Neither faints nor is weary. His understanding is unsearchable. He gives power to the weak, And to those who have no might He increases strength. Even the youths shall faint and be weary, And the young men shall utterly fall, But those who wait on the LORD Shall

renew their strength; They shall mount up with wings like eagles, They shall run and not be weary, They shall walk and not faint." (Isaiah 40:28-31)

Symptoms Of Burnout

In the same way that many physical ailments can be accurately detected, burnout can be accurately diagnosed, prevented, and cured. Every work that we do takes something from us: physical energy, mental energy, emotional energy, etc. If virtue keeps leaving us without being replenished, there will be an imbalance; imbalance is very dangerous. Sadly, some people have been living in a constant state of burnout.

People who are burnt out experience more fear and anger, are short-tempered, are disillusioned, are always discouraged, get disappointed easily, and cannot pray, read the word or worship God. Do you see that this is a very dangerous state to be in? If you are always serving others without being served, you are risking burnout. If you are always working without resting, you are risking burnout. The state of burnout is what many parents, especially of younger children, are always experiencing but are often unable to articulate.

How to Stay Recharged

There are practices you can engage in, to stay afloat and never experience burnout. However, if you are already in a state of burnout, these practices are also applicable, to get you back on track as quickly as possible.

Worship

One day, I was heading home from work when God asked me a question. He asked me, *"Do you know why I am neither tired nor weary?"* Of course, I said no. I have learned that whenever God asks me a question, He knows I do not have the answer. He told me, *"He is neither tired nor weary, because there is always anointed praise and worship where He is."*

The four living creatures, each having six wings, were full of eyes around and within. And they do not rest day or night, saying: "Holy, holy, holy, Lord God Almighty, who was and is and is to come!" Whenever the living creatures give glory and honor and thanks to Him who sits on the throne, who lives forever and ever, the twenty-four elders fall down before Him who sits on the throne and worship Him who lives forever and ever, and cast their crowns before the throne, saying: "You are worthy, O Lord, to receive glory and honor and power; for You created all things, and by Your will they exist and were created." (Revelation 4:8-11)

He told me, *"If I can always be in an atmosphere of anointed praise and worship, my strength will always be renewed."* I have attempted to do this as often as I can, and it has never failed me. I ensure that I have anointed worship playing, especially during very busy and intensive periods.

Meditate On The Word

Another way to stay recharged is to meditate on Scriptures. The Word of God has nutrients that have the power to transform into energy for your spirit, soul and body (Proverbs 4:20-22).

It is a known fact that the sun's light is a key ingredient in photosynthesis. It can also be transformed into energy. Likewise, the Word of God is light (Psalms 119:105), and it can be transformed into tangible energy for the believer to use.

The Scriptures I am referring to are those that have deep meanings to you. Learn to keep track of Bible verses that have ministered powerfully to you in the past, refer to them regularly, and most especially when you are feeling burnt out.

Adequate Rest And Relaxation

Rest and relaxation do not necessarily mean sleeping or going on a vacation. They also do not necessarily mean being idle. Most of the time, when people experience burnout, they immediately begin to think that all they need is a vacation. The truth is that vacations are just being marketed as such. Some vacations leave you more stressed than before the vacation. You sometimes end up going over your budget, which then leads to even more stress.

Rest and relaxation means doing something different from what you have always done. It means taking a break from your work to do something else. Rest and relaxation can be found in reading, sleeping, reflecting on past victories, reflecting on memorable events, etc.

The fact that you are pursuing your vision does not mean that you cannot do something else. Learn a musical instrument, start dancing, or take up painting. Ensure that your vision does not completely consume your entire life. I get more ideas when I take time off from running with the vision to do other productive tasks that are not necessarily in line with the vision.

Praying In The Holy Spirit

Praying in tongues is another way to renew ourselves. We are advised in Jude 1:20, *"But you, beloved, building yourselves up on your most holy faith, praying in the Holy Spirit."* The more we pray in tongues, the more we build ourselves and increase our capacity to withstand the pressures of life.

Apostle John G. Lake had a phenomenal ministry, and one of his secrets was that he always prayed in tongues.

Fasting

Fasting not only renews the body but also every other aspect of man. A person who fasts regularly will always experience inexplicable strength. Even medical science has caught onto the medicinal benefits of fasting. We see these benefits in Isaiah 58:8, 11.

"Then your light shall break forth like the morning, your healing shall spring forth speedily, and your righteousness shall go before you; the glory of the LORD shall be your rear guard." (Isaiah 58:8)

"The LORD will guide you continually, And satisfy your soul in drought, And strengthen your bones; You shall be like a watered garden, And like a spring of water, whose waters do not fail." (Isaiah 58:11)

Revisit The Vision

A visionary is usually most energetic when they receive the vision. They are super pumped and confidently believe in the actualization of the vision. Unfortunately, many people do not go back to read the vision after they have taken off to execute it.

Whenever you go back to read the vision you are running with, especially in the original form where you initially wrote it, a new surge of life comes upon you. This is why God gave Habakkuk the instruction to write the vision down.

Then the LORD answered me and said: "Write the vision And make it plain on tablets, That he may run who reads it." (Habakkuk 2:2)

Every time you read the vision that God gave you, it causes you to get running again.

Perseverance

Perseverance is a virtue that causes you to hold on despite the challenges you face. A person who perseveres is patient and has endurance. Can you hold onto the vision, even when you are not experiencing any success, just because God gave you the vision?

No vision speaks in the beginning. There is no overnight star. Every vision has tears and labour in its roots. The fact that God gave you the vision does not mean that you will not persevere. There is always a waiting period after we have sown seeds. The ground does not yield a harvest immediately a seed is planted; it takes time, and an experienced farmer knows that so well. In fact, the more valuable the seed, the more time it takes before harvest.

Perseverance is the ability to tarry. God said in Habakkuk 2:3, *"For the vision is yet for an appointed time; but at the end it will speak, and it will not lie. Though it tarries, wait for it; Because it will surely come, it will not tarry."* The question for you is, "Will you still be there when the vision will speak or you would have given up?"

"But at the end it will speak" is the same as saying *"at the appointed time, you will receive your harvest."*

True perseverance will make you wait in joy. Perseverance is not the same as complaining while you wait. It is not whether you waited, but how you waited that matters. True perseverance is always accompanied by joy.

"Strengthened with all might, according to His glorious power, for all patience and longsuffering with joy." (Colossians 1:11)

In the current world system that encourages instant gratification, patience and perseverance are foreign words. This is not so in the Word of God. The Bible even tells us, *"For you have need of endurance, so that after you have done the will of God, you may receive the promise"* (Hebrews 10:36). This means that even though you might have sown the seed of diligence if you are not patient, you will never obtain the promise.

When you are pursuing the vision, and you do not see the results you expect, conduct a proper analysis and make the necessary changes, if any. If you conclude that you are doing everything right, continue to joyfully do what is required of you. In the end, you will be victorious.

May God help you discern the difference between enforcing your faith to receive the promise now and patiently waiting for the fulfillment of God's promise.

Prudence

Prudence is the opposite of simplicity. Simplicity, in this context, is the inability to consider complexity when making decisions. A prudent person is capable of making sound decisions because they are not myopic in their thinking. A prudent person does not get overwhelmed by all they have to consider before they make decisions, while a simpleton makes decisions without deep considerations. A prudent person is a deep thinker. God is prudent because His decisions consider a host of factors.

In many cases, factors involved in decision-making are related in a web-like manner (i.e. interdependent), not a simple one-on-one relationship.

A prudent person is careful. They avoid rash behaviour or speech. They can show tact and wisdom in managing the resources at their disposal.

For example, a prudent person always thinks in a sustainable manner. God did not create man, only to realize that there was no food for man to eat. Prudent people think about the long-term consequences of their actions. A sustainable decision takes into consideration, how what you are building will function on its own with minimal supervision, where necessary. God made man and woman once. The design was so sustainable that He did not have to make any other person. The ability to make more men and women was inherent in God's original design. Praise God!

Prudence is not the same as overanalysis. A person engaged in overanalysis usually makes no decision, whereas a prudent person makes timely and well-thought-out decisions. For a prudent person, the decision-making process is joyful and not painful; it is faith-driven and not doubt-ridden; and it is done confidently and not fearfully.

You can grow in prudence by asking God for it (James 1:5). You can also learn to think prudently, by asking certain questions about the decisions you are making. This might seem cumbersome in the beginning, but over time, it will become a natural way of thinking. Some of those questions are:

- How does this decision advance the vision?

- Who does this decision affect?

- What else does this vision affect?

- What are the possible implications of this decision?

- Can I handle the consequences of this decision?

- What next steps do I have to take due to this decision?

The above is definitely not a comprehensive list, but it gives you an example of how prudence causes you to think. The benefits from prudence is what caused God to have wisdom by His side during creation.

"The Lord possessed me at the beginning of His way, before His works of old. I have been established from everlasting, from the beginning, before there was ever an earth. When there were no depths I was brought forth, when there were no fountains abounding with water. Before the mountains were settled, before the hills, I was brought forth; while as yet He had not made the earth or the fields, or the primal dust of the world. When He prepared the heavens, I was there, when He drew a circle on the face of the deep, when He established the clouds above, when He strengthened the fountains of the deep, when He assigned to the sea its limit, so that the waters would not transgress His command, when He marked out the foundations of the earth, then I was beside Him as a master craftsman; and I was daily His delight, rejoicing always before Him, rejoicing in His inhabited world, and my delight was with the sons of men." (Proverbs 8:22-31)

From reading Proverbs 8, you can see why the earth has survived misuse, from so many years of carelessness by man. Hence, attempting to build anything without wisdom will cause more harm than good.

Provision

Every vision will need provision for it to succeed. The provision is anything that will enable the vision to be successful. God is the one that makes provision for the vision. A person who enlists in the military force of any country never goes around trying to raise money to buy their military gear. In the same vein, if God enlists you in His service to carry out any assignment on the earth, be rest assured that He will make the necessary provision that you will need.

The provisions you will need for your vision include people, money, reputation, ideas, etc. In essence, God is committed to making everything you will need available to you, before you will need it.

Many people have turned aside to raise money instead of focusing on the vision. This execution booster is completely God's responsibility. The only part we have to play is to ensure that we are doing what God has asked us to do and that we have faith in Him. So long as those two factors are in place, God is completely committed to making provision.

It is important to build faith in God's ability and willingness to provide for the vision. A lack of faith has caused many to fall into the trap of *the love of money*, destroying the vision. Since the best means to build our faith is the Word of God, let us examine two examples from the Bible.

Building the Tabernacle in the Wilderness

The first example is the building of the Tabernacle in the wilderness. God gave Moses the vision to build a Tabernacle in the wilderness. Can you imagine God asking you to build a tabernacle in the wilderness?

"Then Moses called Bezalel and Aholiab, and every gifted artisan in whose heart the Lord had put wisdom, everyone whose heart was stirred, to come and do the work. And they received from Moses all the offering which the children of Israel had brought for the work of the service of making the sanctuary. So they continued bringing to him freewill offerings every morning. Then all the craftsmen who were doing all the work of the sanctuary came, each from the work he was doing, and they spoke to Moses, saying, "The people bring much more than enough for the service of the work which the Lord commanded us to do." So Moses gave a commandment, and they caused it to be proclaimed throughout the camp, saying, "Let neither man nor woman do any more work for the offering of the sanctuary." And the people were restrained from bringing, for the material they had was sufficient for all the work to be done—indeed too much." (Exodus 36:2-7)

If God could make provision for a tabernacle in the wilderness, how much more the Church building in that city you live in; how much more the business in a bustling city? Your problem is not that God will not provide, but that you lack the faith needed to believe God for the provision.

In Exodus 35:4-9, we see that Moses had enough faith to ask the people to bring offerings for the work of the tabernacle, as God instructed. It was God that told Moses to ask the people for the offering, it was not Moses' idea. God has told many people where to get the provision needed for the work, but they have refused to go get it, because of lack of faith.

"And Moses spoke to all the congregation of the children of Israel, saying, "This is the thing which the Lord commanded, saying: 'Take from among you an offering to the Lord. Whoever is of a willing heart, let him bring it as an offering to the Lord: gold, silver, and bronze; blue, purple, and scarlet thread, fine linen, and goats' hair; ram skins dyed red, badger skins, and acacia wood; oil for the light, and spices for the anointing oil and for the sweet incense; onyx stones, and stones to be set in the ephod and in the breastplate."

If you want to have more than enough for the vision, make up your mind to completely depend on God for your provision. He is more than enough, and He is too faithful to fail. Do you believe it?

The Temple of God

Another scriptural example is the work to build the temple of God. David came up with the idea and God endorsed it through Nathan the prophet. It was now up to God to make the provision.

Again, in this passage of Scripture, we do not see the visioner sweating to obtain the required resources. God can control the heart of His people (Proverbs 21:1, GW) and cause them to give to you (Luke 6:38). Whenever God is the one moving the heart of the people to give, there is always abundance, and they do it with joy.

"Furthermore King David said to all the assembly: "My son Solomon, whom alone God has chosen, is young and inexperienced; and the work is great, because the temple is not for man but for the Lord God. Now for the house of my God I have prepared with all my might: gold for things to be made of gold, silver for things of silver, bronze for things of bronze, iron for things of iron, wood for things of wood, onyx stones, stones to be set, glistening stones of *various colors, all kinds of precious stones, and marble slabs in abundance. Moreover, because I have set my affection on the house of my God, I have given to the house of my God, over and above all that I have prepared for the holy house, my own special treasure of gold and silver: three thousand talents of gold, of the gold of Ophir, and seven thousand talents of refined silver, to overlay the walls of the houses; the gold for things of gold and the silver for things of silver, and for all kinds of work to be done by the hands of craftsmen. Who then is willing to consecrate himself this day to the Lord?" Then the leaders of the fathers' houses, leaders of the tribes of Israel, the captains of thousands and of hundreds, with the officers over the king's work, offered willingly. They gave for the work of the house of God five thousand talents and ten thousand darics of gold, ten thousand talents of silver, eighteen thousand talents of bronze, and one hundred thousand talents of iron. And whoever had precious stones gave them to the treasury of the house of the Lord, into the hand of Jehiel the Gershonite. Then the people rejoiced, for they had offered willingly, because with a loyal heart they had offered willingly to the Lord; and King David also rejoiced greatly."* (1 Chronicles 29:1-9)

God is faithful in making provision for His vision. In these two examples, it is clear that God only provided when He endorsed the work, and the leader had faith in His ability to provide for it by following the instructions.

Power

Power is the ability to get things done. Power is anything that removes limitations from your path. When in pursuit of the vision, there will be obstacles. Power, not tears, is what is needed to remove the obstacles. No one truly pursued God's vision for their lives and did not encounter daunting resistance. The children of Israel had to fight battles on their way to the promised land; Joseph met with resistance in Potiphar's house; David met with Goliath and Saul on his way to the throne; Daniel met with resistance on his way to becoming great in Babylon, etc.

Instead of constantly crying and whining, empower yourself adequately to destroy every resistance on your way to fulfilling destiny. Instead of complaining about how much people hate you and are against you, instead of complaining about how the system is rigged against you, empower yourself to know how to bring down all the barriers on your path.

The opposite of power is weakness. Proverbs 24:10 makes it clear that *"If you faint in the day of adversity, your strength is small."* This means that if you lost a battle, you might have had strength, but it was not a match for the enemy you faced. The measure of your power is based on the enemy you are facing. Some countries are considered powerful until they are matched against a superpower. This is why Jesus told His disciples in Mark 9:29, that there are some obstacles or opposition that will not give way unless you have generated enough power through fasting and prayer.

Power can be measured in force and endurance. Force is the impact of using our power, while endurance is how long we can last before we are worn out.

It is important to note that we can build up power in every aspect of our being. Since man is made up of spirit, soul and body, we ought to build up power in our spirit, soul and body.

Spiritual Power

Spiritual power is the ability to do what only God can do. It is the ability to function in God's capacity. It is not blasphemy to think this way. Jesus clearly said in John 14:12, *"Most assuredly, I say to you, he who believes in Me, the works that I do he will do also; and greater works than these he will do, because I go to My Father."*

On the way to fulfilling your destiny, there will be spiritual obstacles in your path. Paul said in 1 Corinthians 16:9, *"For a great and effective door has opened to me, and there are many adversaries."* Even the angel of God faced spiritual obstacles on its way to deliver a message to Daniel (Daniel 10:13).

We need spiritual power, because every time God's plan begins to unfold, the enemy gets to work, trying to foil it. When Jesus was born, and His birth was announced by God, the devil immediately initiated a plan for Him to be killed (Matthew 2:1-15). When Moses was born, the devil immediately initiated a plan to kill him (Exodus 1:15-22).

Engaging in spiritual practices like prayer, fasting and studying the word, empowers our spirit.

Mental Power

Mental power is measured by the level of soundness of the mind. A sound mind can receive information, store information and process information correctly.

Just like we exercise our body and spirit to become stronger, we must exercise our mind to become stronger. Romans 12:2 clearly instructs us on what to do: *"Be transformed by the renewing of your mind, that you may prove what is that good and acceptable and perfect will of God."* This means that anybody can renew their mind to make it become a tool for success and not failure.

1 Corinthians 2:16 tells us that we have the mind of Christ. We have also not been given the spirit of fear but of power, love, and a sound mind (2 Timothy 1:7). A sound mind is your divine heritage in Jesus Christ.

Building up the soundness of the mind is simply done by feeding it with information that meets the standard in Philippians 4:8.

"Finally, brethren, whatever things are true, whatever things are noble, whatever things are just, whatever things are pure, whatever things are lovely, whatever things are of good report, if there is any virtue and if there is anything praiseworthy—meditate on these things."

Process that information diligently by asking the right kind of questions. Finally, make every effort to document the result from the processing activity and refer to it as often as possible. Back up every step with faith in God's word and declaring that a sound mind is your portion.

Emotional Power

Emotional power is simply the ability to love whoever needs to be loved. This includes God, ourselves, and others. 2 Timothy 1:7 confirms that we have not been given the spirit of fear but of love. Romans 5:5 also says, *"The love of God has been poured out in our hearts by the Holy Spirit who was given to us."*

There are two distinct examples where emotional power was displayed. One was by Jesus Christ (Luke 23:26-34) and the other by Stephen (Acts 7:54-60). They were both able to ask God to forgive those who crucified and stoned them, respectively. The amazing thing about these incidents is that they both forgave right in the midst of the pain they were experiencing.

As you pursue the vision, you will be hurt, disappointed, falsely accused, and attacked. Emotional power will enable you to forgive people easily and quickly so your connection with God is not severed.

The main way to build emotional power is to display love. The more love you display, the more your emotional power is enhanced. It will be difficult to display love by forgiving, but always remember that the more you do it, the easier it will become.

Will Power

This is the ability to make a decision and abide by it. Will is a person's decision-making aspect. The mind performs the analysis, but the will makes the decision and causes you to stick to it.

Throughout the life of your vision, you will make at least hundreds of thousands of decisions. A strong will will allow you to make decisions and abide by them, regardless of the challenges. I have been under the leadership of indecisive leaders, and I have seen the damage they have caused to the morale of the team and the fulfilment of the vision. You do not want to be an indecisive leader.

A strong will is what will ensure that you never give up or surrender, no matter the strength of your opposition. Just like Blind Bartimaeus (Mark 10:46-52), a strong will is what will ensure you never stop until you get what you are looking for. It is a strong will that will make you declare like Esther (Esther 4:16), "if I perish, I perish."

The main way to build up willpower is to agree with every instruction from God, either through Scripture or revelation, and decide to obey it. Do you see why the devil will always convince you that you are unable to do what God says you should do? It is because the devil knows that the more you decide to obey God, the easier it will be for you to obey God until you reach a point where you are constantly obeying God. Even if you do not have any reason to believe you can obey God, just make that decision, and the Holy Spirit will enable you.

Physical Power

This is the lowest type of power a person can have. It is the power that resides in the human body. Even though it is the lowest kind of power, it is still vital that we are physically capable of fulfilling the vision.

Building up physical power involves eating right, exercising, and adopting healthy practices. When all these things are done, and you still don't enjoy good health, pray to God. God can deal with the root cause so you can enjoy physical strength and vitality.

The Bible tells us in Deuteronomy 34:7 that, *"Moses was one hundred and twenty years old when he died. His eyes were not dim nor his natural vigor diminished."* Moses needed physical power to climb mountains, walk for hours, etc. I declare strength to every part of your ailing body now, in Jesus' name!

Passion

What gas is to a car is what passion is to a vision. Passion fuels a vision. It is the excitement that you exude and spread while pursuing your God-given vision. Passion is present when your heart is involved in the pursuit of your vision. Where passion is absent, there is no drive.

Without passion, you will not be able to attract people to join you in implementing the vision. The passion with which Jesus Christ preached attracted the disciples to Him. Also, the passion of John the Baptist attracted disciples to him.

There are times when your level of passion will reduce in the pursuit of your vision; don't be alarmed by this. As passion fuels the vision, so does inspiration fuel passion. There are various sources of inspiration that you can draw from regularly to pursue your vision passionately.

Fuelled by Love

Another major source of passion is love. When you run with the vision because of your love for God, humanity, and yourself, you will be tapping into an unquenchable source of passion. This is because love never fails (1 Corinthians 13:8).

A vision fuelled by money, power, fame, etc. will be short-lived. However, a vision fuelled by love is always focused on the benefits of the vision to the people God has sent you to.

Nehemiah was passionate about his assignment because it was fuelled by love. He did not enjoy any personal benefit because of the work he undertook. In fact, he gave more to the people than he received from them.

"Moreover, from the time that I was appointed to be their governor in the land of Judah, from the twentieth year until the thirty-second year of King Artaxerxes, twelve years, neither I nor my brothers ate the governor's provisions. But the former governors who were before me laid burdens on the people, and took from them bread and wine, besides forty shekels of silver. Yes, even their servants bore rule over the people, but I did not do so, because of the fear of God. Indeed, I also continued the work on this wall, and we did not buy any land. All my servants were gathered there for the work. And at my table were one hundred and fifty Jews and rulers, besides those who came to us from the nations around us. Now that which was prepared daily was one ox and six choice sheep. Also fowl were prepared for me, and once every ten days an abundance of all kinds of wine. Yet in spite of this I did not demand the governor's provisions, because the bondage was heavy on this people. Remember me, my God, for good, according to all that I have done for this people." (Nehemiah 5:14-19)

When your vision is fuelled by love, you will discover that you give more than you receive. Accepting is not a sin, but if you are receiving more than you are giving, there is no love present.

When running with God's vision for our lives, we must be consumed by love. Anything love-driven (the love of God) will never fail.

Fuelled by Purpose

We mentioned earlier that purpose answers the "why" question. When you remain connected to the "why" of your vision, you will remain passionate about it. In fact, you might never need to be encouraged.

There is something unique about purpose-driven visionaries; they are passionate people. As the vision progresses, remain connected to your purpose. Why did you embark on the vision in the first instance? What made you pursue this dream? Your purpose must always remain fixed in your heart.

As a Church founder, my purpose, as delivered by God, is to partner with Him *"to bring about restoration and transformation to all."* So long as someone is still yet to be restored and transformed, I will be passionate about the vision God has given me. Another "why" for me is that I want to hear the words, *"Well done, thou good and faithful servant,"* when my time on earth is over and I stand before God in judgement.

Jesus Christ stated His purpose, time and time again, during His earthly ministry. Here are a few examples:

- *"I have come that they may have life, and that they may have it more abundantly."* (John 10:10)

- *"He who sins is of the devil, for the devil has sinned from the beginning. For this purpose the Son of God was manifested, that He might destroy the works of the devil."* (1 John 3:8)

- *"The Spirit of the Lord is upon Me, because He has anointed Me to preach the gospel to the poor; He has sent Me to heal the brokenhearted, to proclaim liberty to the captives and recovery of sight to the blind, to set at liberty those who are oppressed."* (Luke 4:18)

When your purpose is well-fixed in your heart, you will naturally be passionate. Even though you get tired, you will not remain tired.

Fuelled by Stories of Overcomers

The Bible contains stories of overcomers. They are people who fulfilled their vision against all odds. Hebrews 11 lists many of those overcomers. The more you read about people who encountered worse situations than you and prevailed, the more you will be inspired to press on to the end.

You can also find stories of non-Bible characters who made a positive mark on the world. Let their stories inspire you to be your best every single day of your life. Open your heart to healthy inspiration from as many sources as possible to keep your passion for the vision burning.

9
Goal Planning Template

THANKSGIVING

Thanksgiving must precede any planning process - thank God for the highs & the lows

20XX (CURRENT YEAR) REVIEW

Take a holistic approach to this - **spiritual, mental, emotional, will, physical, financial, family, career**

What went well?

What could have been improved?

What hindered you the most this year?

What goals were achieved & why?

What goals were not achieved & why?

20XX (CURRENT YEAR) GRADE

Come up with a pass mark - the goal is not for pride or condemnation, but so you are properly balanced

Remember: progress not perfection

Areas that need more focus

20XX (NEW YEAR) VISION

Lord, what is the plan for next year?

Ensure that these are specific goals

- State what you will AND/OR will not do, and avoid making outrageous goals

- For each goal, consider: What, How, When, Where, and Why?

Spiritual

- Where do you see yourself at the end of the new year spiritually

Soul

Mental

- Anything that will improve/affect your mental state

Emotional

- Emotional intelligence: Self-awareness, Self-regulation, Empathy, Motivation, Social skills

Will

- The decision making aspect of the soul; discipline, self-control

Physical

- Health: diet, exercise

Financial

- Savings, investments, budgeting, debt repayment

Relationships

- Family, friends, church community, romantic

Career

- Ministry, Career/Business, academics, extracurriculars

EXECUTION

How will I achieve this vision; what will you do & who will you consult?

Consultation

Who will I contact to advise me to get to these goals?

Timeline

Programming - schedule it & put it in your calendar

January

February

March

April

May

June

July

August

September

October

November

December

Accountability

Put systems in place to keep you accountable to your goals: quarterly or monthly reviews, retreats, touch base with mentors/consultants

Epilogue

Now that you have absorbed the anointed words in this book, step forward with confidence, knowing that you are equipped with the essential tools to fulfill the vision God has given you.

My friend, please take the appropriate steps to receive God's vision for your life. Commit yourself to paying the price to implement that vision. Avoid the pitfalls where others have fallen. Engage the execution boosters that will take the vision to the extent God intended.

As you pursue the vision, refer to this book and other anointed materials that will boost your confidence in your God-given ability to execute like a pro.

See you at the top!

Contact the Author

I know without a doubt that this book has been a blessing to you. I am looking forward to hearing your testimony.

You can stay connected with me through the following platforms:

Instagram: e.adewusi | **Youtube:** Emmanuel Adewusi
Website: emmanueladewusi.org

SUPPORT THE AUTHOR

Review the Book

A Sinner's Prayer

Dear Heavenly Father,

I come to You in the Name of Jesus Christ.

You said in Your Word, "Whosoever shall call upon the name of the Lord shall be saved." (Romans 10:13) I am calling on Your Name, so I know You have saved me now.

You also said that "if you confess with your mouth the Lord Jesus and believe in your heart that God has raised Him from the dead, you will be saved. For with the heart one believes unto righteousness, and with the mouth, confession is made unto salvation." (Romans 10:9-10) I believe in my heart Jesus Christ is the Son of God. I believe that He was raised from the dead for my justification, and I confess Him now as my Lord and Savior.

Thank you, Lord, because now, I am saved!

Thank You, Lord, because I know you have heard my prayer. Thank You, Lord, because I am now born again.

Signed _____

Date _____

About the Author

Apostle Emmanuel Adewusi is the Founding and Lead Pastor of Cornerstone Christian Church of God.

Called into ministry with the mandate to "bring restoration and transformation to all by teaching, preaching, and demonstrating the Gospel of Jesus Christ," he is passionate about seeing lives restored and transformed as God intended from the beginning of creation. He has a zeal for the full counsel of the Word of God, fellowship with the Holy Spirit, and being under spiritual authority.

He authored the books *"Now That You Are Born Again, What Next?"*, *"The Blessings of Being Under Spiritual Authority," "A Disciplined Life," "The Enlightened Believer," "The Skilled Sower,"* and other impactful titles. He has also released an album titled *"Divine Encounter"* and many more on the way.

Emmanuel Adewusi is joyfully married to his wife, Ibukun Adewusi, and together, they are building a thriving Christ-centered family.

www.ingramcontent.com/pod-product-compliance
Lightning Source LLC
Chambersburg PA
CBHW071146060526
44107CB00132B/267